Liste
to the Soul

Sandra Holt is a former computer programmer and lecturer living in rural Aberdeenshire where her husband is minister to a Church of Scotland congregation. An experienced spiritual director, Sandra divides her time between writing, guiding people through the Spiritual Exercises of Ignatius of Loyola, and working with the Church of Scotland's Board of Ministry in the selection and training process for ministers. In her spare time Sandra acts as taxi-driver for her three busy children. She is the author of *Intimacy Human and Divine*, also published by SPCK.

Listening to the Soul

Sandra Holt

First published in Great Britain in 2002 by
Society for Promoting Christian Knowledge
Holy Trinity Church
Marylebone Road
London NW1 4DU

British Library Cataloguing-in-Publication Data
A catalogue record for this book is available from the British Library

ISBN 0–281–05459–2

Typeset by Pioneer Associates, Perthshire
Printed in Great Britain by
Bookmarque Ltd, Croydon, Surrey

*To all those who have allowed me
the privilege of listening to their soul*

Contents

1

What God has in Mind

Long before he laid down earth's foundations,
he had us in mind,
had settled on us as the focus of his love,
to be made whole and holy by his love.

(Ephesians 1.4, Peterson, 1993)

What is it that God has in mind for you? Or, to put it another way, do you know who you are, why you are here, and what path in life will make you wholly content? Not many of us do. And yet these are the very questions God is concerned with on our behalf. They concern us too, of course. When we are young we wonder what we will be when we grow up. As teenagers we ponder which path to take out of secondary education. In our thirties we look again at the choices we have made so far and, in the light of experience, perhaps consider making new choices. In middle years a panic can set in: half our life is over and there rises within us a sense of urgency for the second half to be meaningful and authentic. And so life goes on. Who we are, what our life means, and how to live it happily: these questions are always on our mind. Not because we are human, but because we are divine.

You see, we are on God's mind. We are the focus of a love

1

intent on creating each one of us 'in his own image' (Genesis 1.27). I think this means that God has in mind for each of us a unique and irreplaceable identity that will make us whole, and therefore holy. A personal identity that will answer all our questions of who, and what, and where, and why – freeing us from many unnecessary concerns to offer the world our true selves. And I believe this is something of a passion with the Creator. So much so, in fact, that all the energy of the universe is focused on it. Most of the time we do not notice the energy or the passion. We are too busy doing lots of different things to pay attention to whether or not those things reflect who we truly are and what God has in mind for us and for our world. But just sometimes we may catch a glimpse of God's providence behind a 'happy coincidence' or God's energy behind nature. Regardless of whether or not we are 'religious', we momentarily sense that the truth about ourselves, our world and the Creator of it all is greater and more integrated than we have yet understood or can imagine.

For months his school drama teacher had been telling me that my son had an extraordinary natural ability for acting. I knew this of course, or thought I did, because Jonathan often has the entire family helpless with laughter as he depicts a scene from ordinary life in comic but closely observed mime. Then came the first time I saw him act on stage in a production of *Godspell*: Jonathan was cast as Judas, and I left the theatre shaken. Certainly I was thrilled for my son, but to watch his performance was more than thrilling. It was to watch a young man fully alive and completely at home in his own skin. It was to glimpse God's passion and glory alive and joyfully active, burning brightly, but without consuming the personality I knew as my son. Holy ground indeed.

I am reminded of the story of a little boy who watches a sculptor at work on a huge piece of marble. The sculptor works silently, the boy watches from an upturned bucket, the days go by. At last the work is complete. The sculptor stands back, tools lying still in his hands. A proud and magnificent lion looks down from the marble at the boy and the artist. As the boy gazes up at it he asks: 'How did you know the lion was in there?'

How indeed. The rock and the sculptor are connected by what the sculptor sees in his mind and can produce with his skilled hands. Our passage from Ephesians at the beginning of this Chapter tells me that long before my son was born, God knew him as that sculptor knew his lion. God has always had an image of Jonathan in mind; has always seen him whole and holy – a once-in-a-universe creation. He is an unrepeatable expression of divine activity, albeit a work still in progress. The same is true of you and of me.

But you and I are not blocks of stone. The stuff God is working with, and from which our true identity must emerge, is flesh and blood, personality and will. We can question our Creator and place conditions on our co-operation with the artist's work. And because each of us is a restless mixture of nature and nurture, of instinctive responses and complex relationships, we do both. God labours with it all; with faith and with doubts, with a person's temperament and history, with our desires and with our ambivalence.

God labours patiently, lovingly, skilfully in all the circumstances of our lives, to make us wholly the creation he/she has in mind, and we find ourselves drawn, at least some of the time, to assist. For some of the time we want very much to co-operate in the task of freeing our truest and most authentic selves from the stone that keeps our divinity hidden like a diamond in the rough.

To work out our own identity in God, which the Bible

calls 'working out our salvation', is a labour that requires
sacrifice and anguish, risk and many tears. It demands
close attention to reality at every moment, and great
fidelity to God as He reveals Himself, obscurely, in the
mystery of each new situation. We do not know clearly
beforehand what the result of this work will be. The
secret of my full identity is hidden in Him. He alone can
make me who I am, or rather who I will be when at last
I fully begin to be. (Merton, 1972)

The secret of my full identity is hidden in God, and often I
am at a loss to know how to co-operate with the work he is
doing in me. Working out that salvation is what this book is
about. It is for those who want to discover the discoverable
and are prepared to roll up their sleeves to labour alongside
God in the task of uncovering the divine image in them. It is
also and necessarily a book about Jesus of Nazareth.

Jesus was a man who wanted to know who he was, why
he was, and what direction his life should take. He had to
discover these things in much the same way as we do. Jesus
had to work out his own identity in God, and so well do
Merton's words capture this experience that they could have
been spoken by Jesus himself.

Perhaps this is a new idea for you. Without meaning to,
we can project our own faith in, and knowledge of, the risen
Christ on to the Gospel stories of Jesus as an infant, an adolescent, and a young man. We imagine he always knew who he
was, why he was, and what his life would mean. But I suggest
that the baby lying in Bethlehem's manger could not have
understood any of this. I think the 12-year-old Jesus astounded
the Temple elders by the depth of his questions regarding
the Law rather than by the width of his knowledge (though
I am reminded of a postcard with the recommendation

'Quick, ask a teenager while they still know everything'). And I believe that the young man working in his father's carpentry shop came *gradually* to suspect that making wooden furniture for his neighbours in Nazareth was not, after all, the family business.

Jesus had to discover who he was, and why, in much the same way as we all do: bit by bit and with plenty of opportunity for incredulity, doubt, even denial. At least this is what the gospel tells me when I read: 'And Jesus increased in wisdom, in stature, and in favour with God and men' (Luke 2.52). We can unwittingly overlook this good news when we put our deep confidence in the divinity of the Son, failing to reflect or even notice that Jesus was the Son made *man* for our sake. That like us:

> He grew; he changed; he learned; he made human mistakes. Writings of modern theologians on the notion of the emerging messianic consciousness of Christ are not always clear. What is clear is an idea seen as early as Cyril of Alexandria. The Jesus of Nazareth who learns as we do, who learns by groping, who must apparently, as we shall later see, agonize over religious decisions, this is a Jesus with whom today's Christian can identify most easily. (Sheehan, 1978)

The task of growing into his unique and irreplaceable identity demanded the same kind of things of Jesus that it will demand from us. Like Jesus, we must want to know who we are before God and be willing to work at this discovery. Then we need to pay close attention to the reality of our ordinary daily experience, and nurture within ourselves fidelity towards the God who reveals himself, usually obscurely, in the mystery of each unfolding situation. And we too must be prepared to learn by groping, by making choices, taking risks, and confronting our mistakes. This, after all, is what it means to be human.

But an encounter with the humanity of Jesus can be discomforting. Even now you may be aware of a number of reactions within yourself to the idea of Jesus having to work out his own identity. These may strike you in any order: unease or anger, distress or perhaps disbelief, mild interest or a suggestion of relief, even hope. Take your time. Let this new idea stay with you for the rest of the day. Treat it as you would a distant and never-before-met cousin who turns up at your door – vaguely familiar, but at the same time a stranger. Try to be as hospitable as you can for at least a day, turning the idea over in your mind. After that, you can decide whether this new arrival can stay longer or should be sent packing. Perhaps these lines from Gerard Manley Hopkins will assist your reflections. They may even capture something of the hopefulness I hope you come to feel:

> I am all at once what Christ is, since he was what I am,
>   and
> This Jack joke, poor potsherd, patch, matchwood,
>   immortal diamond,
> Is immortal diamond.

(Hopkins, 1982)

I am immortal diamond, but not just me and not in isolation. A well-cut diamond, the kind that lives forever in men's imaginations, has many connecting surfaces. As I hope this book will make clear, it is not just the individual, but the whole of humanity, that God focuses on with loving energy and total commitment. My uniqueness is but one facet of the holiness God has in mind.

Now if Jesus was what I am, then Sheehan is right. This is a man with whom we can easily identify, and the story of Jesus in the gospel is a most useful one to spend time contemplating in prayer. In prayer, by the grace of God labouring for me, I will surely find connections between his life and the one I am living. The discoveries Jesus made as a boy and as a man may facilitate my own. His deep trust in God's care and nearness may nurture a similar trust in me, and his total commitment to authenticity, even in the face of agonizing decisions, may inspire and challenge the direction of my life.

If you are familiar with my earlier book, *Intimacy Human and Divine*, you may recall that when I needed help to identify the connections between my life and Christ's I was introduced to the Spiritual Exercises of Ignatius of Loyola. Ignatius lived some 500 years ago and developed an introduction to prayer that has proved to be a valuable devotional approach both to the gospel and to the human psyche. I am still using this introduction to contemplative prayer both personally and with other people who want to become aware of their God-given uniqueness, and to live out of that identity in growing freedom and truth.

In this present book I do not intend to lead the reader through the complete set of exercises; those interested can seek out an Ignatian retreat centre, and one or two helpful websites are given at the end of this chapter. I will, however, give a taste of what the Spiritual Exercises offer as I try to help you make connections between the life of Jesus – his actions and interactions, words and deeds – and your own. As Ignatius suggests, we will use our imagination to accompany Jesus from the manger to maturity and beyond. We will watch carefully as he recognizes that God is the giver of life, look for the moment when he chooses to follow a hunch about his own authentic and unrepeatable identity, notice how he works out his own salvation in his actions, choices and encounters with others.

Contemplating the gospel is about looking for God in an encounter that takes place between the message written down so long ago and the messages of my own ordinary daily experiences of life. To allow this encounter to happen it will be important to observe two things. First, that: '. . . the Gospels were, to some extent, a new and special kind of literature. They are a mixture of factual accuracy, imaginative development and interpretive reflection, undertaken to evoke and sustain faith in Jesus as God's messenger' (Forward, 1998).

Knowing this allows us to add our imaginations to those of the Gospel writers. We can flesh out the stories they have recorded, develop them in a way personal to our own concerns, and so evoke a new depth of faith in Jesus as the Word of God to us.

Second, we should keep in mind the inspiration behind all Scripture: that it is God-breathed. It 'cuts like any double-edged sword but more finely: it can slip through the place where the soul is divided from the spirit, or joints from the marrow; it can judge the secret emotions and thoughts' (Hebrews 4.12). God has chosen, and is able, to reveal divine intention and meaning (what God has in mind) through the message of Scripture as it was spoken, remembered, half-forgotten, paraphrased, written down, copied, mis-copied, translated, and passed on from one generation to the next.

Attending to both these points will help us approach contemplation of the gospel with appropriate respect and availability, allowing us to discover that '. . . the creative imagination may plumb truths that mere facts never could' (Forward, 1998).

One final point needs to be made before we begin. The one who grew into the realization of himself as the Christ can, 2000 years on, help you discover that image of the divine that God sees when God sees you. He is more than willing to do so. But you, of course, must want this. Contemplating the life of Jesus and making connections, through robust reflection, with our own lives and the choices we make, can lead us to the truth about our irreplaceable selves. However, merely observing another soul will not facilitate the discovery of my own. Watching my son fully alive on the stage can only prompt me to discover where I am most fully alive; it is no substitute for this discovery. So I must enlist God's help to transform each insight that both life and Scripture offer me into something more 'alive and active' (Hebrews 4.12). Imagining a scene from the gospel is not prayer unless I am also praying for the grace I need to co-operate with the Spirit of the Artist patiently at work in all the details of my life and being.

So begin by spending some time asking in prayer for the one thing necessary – I believe this to be the ability to see Jesus more clearly. Make this short prayer part of your daily routine, offering it as you rise from bed: 'Grant me the grace to see Jesus more clearly in this day.' And each time you read a passage from Scripture with the intention of reflecting upon it, ask for the grace to see Jesus more clearly in what you are reading.

Ignatius was convinced that a person who sees Jesus will inevitably find himself/herself attracted to his humanity, and in being attracted will want to follow him. So it was for the two disciples of John who accompanied Jesus home for a day, just to see where he lived. Our task is also the discovery of where Jesus lives, because where he lives in us will tell us where we are most truly alive.

In addition to this simple prayer, and if you are already at the point of wanting to be wholly available to whatever God has in mind for you as a unique and irreplaceable gift to the cosmos, the words of this hymn, spoken as a prayer or sung, may also be helpful:

> Take my life, and let it be
> consecrated, Lord, to Thee;
> take my moments and my days,
> let them flow in ceaseless praise.
>
> Take my hands, and let them move
> at the impulse of Thy love;
> take my feet, and let them be
> swift and beautiful for Thee.
>
> Take my voice, and let me sing
> always, only, for my King;
> take my lips, and let them be
> filled with messages from Thee.
>
> Take my silver and my gold,
> not a mite would I withhold;
> take my intellect, and use
> every power as Thou shalt choose.
>
> Take my will, and make it Thine;
> it shall be no longer mine:
> take my heart, it is Thine own;
> it shall be Thy royal throne.
>
> Take my love; my Lord I pour
> at Thy feet its treasure store;
> take myself, and I will be
> ever, only, all for Thee.
>
> (Havergal, 1975)

The step from 'let me see Jesus' to the words of this hymn can seem like a big one. Don't worry if you do not feel ready to declare yourself wholly available to God at present. In fact, none of us is totally convinced that life would be inestimably better and more meaningful if we placed all our rich selves – body, mind and spirit – at God's disposal. The most devoted of us is ambivalent, and we will look at some of the reasons why in the following chapters. Thankfully, the efficacy of a prayer does not depend solely on the amount of feeling the praying person can put into it. Even if you detect a certain amount of reservation, you may still resolve to pray these words of offering as though your only desire is to be wholly available to God's will for you. This in itself is an offering of your entire will, and quite correctly depends on the grace of God to fill in the gap between where you are and where you would like to be.

You can work alongside God in this matter by taking some time to discover what the words of each verse mean for you and the life you are living. Moments and days that flow in ceaseless praise may seem fine as an idea, but what are the practical implications for you? And notice that things become a little more challenging in the fourth verse of the hymn – 'my silver and my gold' – or, as Ignatius might pray: 'all that I have, all that I possess' (Fleming, 1978). Our intellects, power, wills, and the very heart of our beings are parts we rarely, if ever, feel inclined to hand over to anyone. So consider what it might mean for you to hand these over to God. Is there comfort for you in the prospect – or discomfort? What is the grace you need to make this offering a possibility?

Be assured that we all have some difficulties with the idea of co-operating with God's dream of wholeness and holiness. This is partly because the image we have of God is not in itself entirely wholesome, nor is it conducive to confidence and trust in God's concern for our well-being. Often we need the grace of a deep confidence and trust in God's care and nearness before we can approach God with a prayer like the one above without feeling anxious. Jesus can help us here too. By getting to know him more deeply, we come also to know the person of God more truly. And knowing can lead to trusting. So let me show you how to make some of those connections that exist between Christ's life and yours, his choices and your own. By so doing you may discover, like others before you, not only who Jesus is for you, but also who you are for him.

References

Fleming, SJ, David L., *Draw Me Into Your Friendship: The Spiritual Exercises. A Literal Translation and a Contemporary Reading.* St Louis, Institute of Jesuit Sources, 1996.

Forward, Martin, *Jesus: A Short Biography*. Oxford, Oneworld Publications, 1998.

Havergal, Frances Ridley, in *The Church Hymnary*, third edition. London, Oxford University Press, 1975.

Hopkins, Gerard Manley, 'That Nature is a Heraclitean Fire and of the Comfort of the Resurrection', in *The Faber Book of Modern Verse*. London, Faber & Faber, 1982.

Merton, Thomas, *Seeds of Contemplation*. Wheathampstead, Anthony Clarke Books, 1972.

Peterson, Eugene, *The Message*. Colorado, NavPress Publishing Group, 1993.

Sheehan, SJ, John F. X., *On Becoming Whole in Christ*. Chicago, Loyola University Press, 1978.

Websites:

Loyola Hall, Liverpool, England: http://home.clara.net/loyola

St Beuno's Retreat Centre, Wales: http://members.aol.com/StBeunos

Loyola House, Guelph, Canada (Ontario): http://www.jesuits.ca/guelph

2

Announcing the Soul

So Joseph set out from the town of Nazareth in Galilee and travelled up to Judaea, to the town of David called Bethlehem, since he was of David's house and line, in order to be registered together with Mary, his betrothed, who was with child. While they were there the time came for her to have her child, and she gave birth to a son, her first-born. She wrapped him in swaddling clothes, and laid him in a manger because there was no room for them at the inn.

(Luke 2.4–7)

The story of Jesus began, of course, some nine months before that trip to Bethlehem. It began when Mary had a vision, and Joseph had a reassuring dream. 'My soul proclaims the greatness of the Lord' (Luke 1.46) sang Mary. Joseph believed her. I have a hunch that he was wise to do so – because Mary was right: both about having a soul and about its bias towards God.

We all have a soul. Try not to think of yours as some *thing* contained in your body. This can lead to an unhelpful separation of body and soul as though the one were a mere container for the much holier other. It also leads to a fruitless search for the exact location of the holy bit: the ghost in the machine. When we fail to find it we become frustrated, and this can lead to an unnecessary denial of the soul. Actually, all we need to do is widen our area of search.

Matthew Fox helpfully suggests that we should not think of the soul as being in the body at all, but rather of the body being in and part of the soul. I like this idea. From this perspective, my wholeness consists of both my material self and the immaterial. The material self includes those parts that are either visible or observable in some way, like body, mind and personality, or the human spirit. But not all of me is observable or measurable.

Think of an iceberg floating in the water like an island. Only one-third of the iceberg is visible; the rest lies beneath the sea. Not only is this two-thirds hidden from sight, but it is also, at some considerable depth perhaps, connected to other icebergs. These broke off from the mainland and may rejoin before long. The body of the iceberg island I can see is part of this much larger mass of ice.

Or think of cracking open an egg on a flat surface. The yellow of the yoke is there to see surrounded by the white. But this white of the egg seems, in its transparent and runny constituency, less material than the yoke. It can spread out for an infinite distance, as anyone who has accidentally dropped an egg on the floor will know, while still being intrinsically a part of the egg. So it is with a soul. My material self is the nucleus of a larger immaterial me. What is measurable – height, weight, colour of eyes, blood pressure and DNA, along with what is observable by means of personality indicators like Myers-Briggs – assures me of my individuality. The bit that cannot be measured or observed so conveniently not only includes all of this, but also connects me as an individual to other individual souls (or is it eggs and icebergs?) and to God, the Creator of all.

What I sense is that my soul is a connection between me and the Love that is fashioning me. I am most aware of this connection whenever I listen to Mozart or gaze at the majestic hills opposite my home with their ancient trees patiently withstanding every storm, graciously surrendering to each season in turn. I feel it too when I watch a person living out of their uniqueness; experiencing what Jesus called 'life in all its fullness'. In those moments something tells me there is more to a human life than meets the eye, more to this world than the purely material. My soul, like Mary's before me, cannot help but proclaim the greatness of what it sees and feels. That we are all, in spite of the mess our world is in and the hardships we inflict on one another, in some immeasurable way connected to one another and to a good God.

My soul, then, is connected to the soul of Mary and I can learn from her. Mary's soul nurtured and animated her material life to make it uniquely worth living, drawing her attention to God and, perhaps unexpectedly for a young girl of those times and culture, to her unique identity in God. For as she awaited her marriage and prayed for God's blessing on it, Mary heard God speak to her, not just through the Scriptures or through the comfortable homilies of synagogue priests, but directly:

'Rejoice, so highly favoured! The Lord is with you.' She was deeply disturbed by these words and asked herself what this greeting could mean, but the angel said to her, 'Mary, do not be afraid; you have won God's favour. Listen! You are to conceive and bear a son, and you must name him Jesus. He will be great and will be called Son of the Most High. The Lord God will give him the throne of his ancestor David; he will rule over the House of Jacob for ever and his reign will have no end.'

Mary said to the angel, 'But how can this come about, since I am a virgin?' 'The Holy Spirit will come upon you' the angel answered 'and the power of the Most High will cover you with its shadow. And so the child will be holy and will be called Son of God. Know this too: your kinswoman Elizabeth has, in her old age, herself conceived a son, and she whom people called barren is now in her sixth month, for nothing is impossible to God.' 'I am the handmaid of the Lord,' said Mary 'let what you have said be done to me.' (Luke 1.28–38)

Mary listened, and heard God invite her to be the mother of God. It was of course a once-in-a-universe vocation she was being offered but not, I believe, a once-only situation. The story of the annunciation is our story too, and the connection between the soul of Mary and our souls is this: God asks each of us to be the highly favoured one he/she has in mind, visiting each of us with a proclamation of hope, a message of annunciation. You too, be you man or woman, are asked by God to give birth to the Son in some way. You are invited to be the means through which God can break into the world and save it.

Of course we may feel, as Mary did, a bit disturbed by this notion. Certainly we have questions and need to look for confirmation of this bizarre sense we have that God looks upon us in a special way with creative mercy. Though we want to declare ourselves 'the handmaid of the Lord' as generously as Mary did, yet we fear being foolish and this fear may keep us silent. We do not speak about the vision our souls have for our life. Perhaps we cannot see that it makes any sense in our present situation; like Mary, we ask: 'How can this come about?' But, unlike Mary, we remain unconvinced by our angel, unconnected with our truest, deepest self, and disengaged from the salvific work that will give meaning and purpose to our lives. If only we could think to check out what we are hearing; speak to someone with experience of what we are going through. Mary did just that.

In the days before pregnancy tests, Mary beetled off to see her kinswoman Elizabeth for confirmation of both the pregnancy and its significance. It was a good choice and a wise angel that sent her. Elizabeth herself was already six months pregnant with a child she had long ago given up hope of conceiving. She had already gone through those early stages of disbelief, of 'How can this be?', the uncertainty of 'Am I or aren't I?' Against all the odds, considering her age, Elizabeth had safely carried the multiplying cells of new life through the first vulnerable weeks and now her expectancy was clearly visible to all. She could offer reassurance to Mary, and some welcome company during the weeks of waiting and watching that lay ahead for both of them.

Mary visited Elizabeth for much the same reasons that people visit me. They come to talk to me because they are unsure if they can trust the crazy dream they have begun to dream of a God who asks of them a favour. Like Mary, they come seeking confirmation and, like Elizabeth, I tell them whenever the child in my womb leaps for joy at the sound of their approaching some important truth about God and the life God is conceiving in them.

The name traditionally given for this kind of help is spiritual direction. A spiritual director is a Christian trained to listen, ask a useful question, and give encouragement to someone seeking to listen to their own soul in order to know self more truly and know God more dynamically.

Now you may not have access at present to a spiritual director, or even feel sure that you want one. That is OK. Allow me to offer what help I can as we contemplate together the story of Jesus. We will become attentive, as he was and his mother before him, to what the soul of every human being proclaims about God. Together we will look for connections between his story and our own ordinary experience. Jesus discovered who he was and why, and he can help us to do the same if we check out what our souls are telling us with what his soul told him.

Then we too will discover that every soul proclaims the greatness of God. How could it be otherwise? Those who learn to listen to their souls always hear a proclamation of God's goodness. Like Mary, they count themselves blessed, recognizing the great things that God has done for them and the service God asks of them.

Of course the possibility has to be faced that Mary was wrong. And if Mary was wrong about the soul, then all the canonized saints – including Ignatius and the ordinary saints such as Merton – are wrong, and I am wrong too, and reading this book is a waste of your time. Recently I watched a celebrity being interviewed about her life and work as an entertainer. She said that for her it was just childish arrogance to imagine any meaning to life. From her own experience and the experience of people in general, she concluded that it was foolish to hope for more from life than was immediately obvious. And it seemed obvious to her that life is fully defined by chemistry, biology and physics – that the events and circumstances produced by these three are arbitrary and as likely to wreak havoc in a life as to bring happiness; and so, this being the case, the sooner we learn to take the rough with the smooth, the less likely we are to suffer disillusionment and despair. This was her personal philosophy for life. And of course she could be right.

Perhaps there is no meaning, no order, no dream of wholeness. With me there has always been room for this kind of doubt. Faith is not a certainty for me, but a strong hunch by which I have chosen to live. I consider that if it really *was* an angel of the Lord who visited Mary that night (and not some cheese she ate for supper re-visiting her), then that visit too left room for doubt; for saying not 'How can this be?' but rather 'This cannot be'. I consider that room for doubt, for a little atheism, is a healthy sign in any numinous or religious experience. In fact, I find myself beginning to twitch nervously at descriptions of people being overtaken by the Holy Spirit in any way that cannot possibly be doubted. If there is a God, then I'm pretty sure (though not certain) that doubt was one of the first freedoms he/she wanted to guarantee humanity.

Of course if my hunch is wrong, and we are here because we have occurred and when we cease to breathe our occurrence will be over, then the trick to life for you, for me, for Jesus, would indeed be to abandon our search for a God-given identity. We should enjoy life while it is smooth, and try not to make matters worse for ourselves by falling into despair when things get rough. If we are not deliberate souls straining to become whole and holy, but instead random occurrences waiting to be extinguished, then the rough and smooth principle is a very sensible philosophy. It is one that has always been popular. However, it remains a philosophy that few, if any, of us seem able to master – and the facts of evolution appear reluctant to confirm. I find that odd.

Even in my most atheistic moments I find it odd that no matter how determinedly we take the rough with the smooth, our souls will not let us rest. Even those of us enjoying the good life of peace, prosperity and personal development are restless. Gurus, gourmets and global communications abound, all offering to enhance our lifestyle. But nothing satisfies. Meanwhile, this rough and smooth and ultimately meaningless life winds on and winds down while we anaesthetize ourselves against the arbitrariness of our good fortune and the inevitability of our bad. Hysterically we become hooked on youth and beauty or anything from coffee to cyber space, heroin to haute couture, while the kind of despair that allows other people's children to starve is everywhere like a plague killing millions. It creeps into our governments, our businesses, our schools and homes, where people file through life not daring even to hope that they are made in the image of a purposeful God. Instead they stumble blindly around destroying God's creation, thwarting God's kind intention, or just simply missing God's meaning.

On balance, I think the question of the soul will not evolve away because it cannot. Creation *is* more than chemistry, physics and biology. The development of a human being involves more than the visible body or the conscious – and therefore observable – mind. At least, this is my hunch. Happily, and I trust significantly, it is a hunch shared by all the great mystics and the majority of scientists in every century; men and women who are unsatisfied with the idea of an accidental life. Scientists like the astrophysicist Herbert D. Curtis, who wrote in the *Los Angeles Times*:

> I personally find it impossible to regard Handel's *Largo*, Keats's 'Ode to a Grecian Urn', and the higher ethics as mere by-products of the chemical interaction of a collection of hydrocarbon molecules. With energy, matter, space, and time continuous, with nothing lost or wasted, are we ourselves the only manifestation that comes to an end, ceases, is annihilated at three score years and ten? (Cousineau, 1995)

I think not. I am not an arbitrary manifestation. I am a soul, here by God's design and for God's delight. The connection between me and the love that fashions me will always be recognizable to God, if not always to me, just as the lion is recognized by the sculptor as part of his life's work, his vision, his very being. Our souls are here to stay because God intends to hold on to the connections he/she is forming with us. In the midst of humanity's desperate games of war and peace, of spoils and victims, soul sense tells us to look beyond our materialism to the immortality God means to share with us.

If you have even the smallest of hunches that you have a soul and that your soul is biased towards God, then re-read the story of Mary's annunciation as though the angel had decided to visit you this day with a message about your personal identity. Reflect on what ways you feel yourself to be the highly favoured one of God. This may take some time, not because of all the ways in which you feel favoured (though I hope there are lots), but because of a resistance we all feel to the notion that we are favoured at all or are in any way special. So be patient and prayerful about this. Ask tentative questions like, 'What might this greeting refer to in my life so far?' When you are ready, move on to notice any early signs of some new possibility being conceived in your life: a change of direction in work or service perhaps, or a persistent desire to re-form your present lifestyle and/or relationships.

The prospect of any kind of change can cause anxiety, just as a flood of hormones in a newly pregnant woman can cause nausea, so notice how your whole self is reacting to the prospect of being available to the living God. Ponder what help you will need from God in order to say with some degree of conviction, 'Let what you have said be done to me' (Luke 1.38). Then make the prayer for the grace you need, and wait patiently for the assurance Joseph received in order to take Mary home as his wife: 'because she has conceived what is in her by the Holy Spirit' (Matthew 1.20).

Reference

Cousineau, P. (ed.), *Soul: An Archaeology*. London, Thorsons, 1995.

3

Out of the Mouths of Babes

The Word was first,
the Word present to God,
God present to the Word.
The Word was God,
In readiness for God from day one.
(John 1.1–2, Peterson, 1993)

This is how John opens his record of the things that happened to and around his friend Jesus from Nazareth. It is a cosmic view he sees and tries to convey; a hymn of creation that is meant to inspire faith in the reader. John is blessed with hindsight, of course, at the point of writing. His Gospel is an exercise in remembering the things he has witnessed, the things he has heard reported, the things he has experienced first-hand and via the reports of others. These memories he draws together in the only way that makes sense to him. His recollections lead him to conclude that the Word with which he opens his Gospel of Jesus Christ is also the Word that opened the very act of creation. This is John's lived experience and future hope, the beginning and the end of his good news, its starting point and goal. He declares that Jesus of Nazareth was and is and always will be the Word; the very meaning uttered by God, as indivisible from the one true and indivisible God as a word of poetry is indivisible from the poet.

The Word, however, came quietly into the world. Mary accepted an invitation to become her true self. This 'yes' of hers took root and grew silently and unseen in her womb until the time was right. Then an infant soul began its journey into life, with experiences common to us all.

Immediately he sensed both warmth and cold, comfort and pain. Later he would sense love and fear, watch adults, and listen to stories. A child learns what he lives. A soul does too. Both the material and the immaterial aspects of a person need security, comforting contact, and a universal welcome – and the sooner these are experienced the better. We only have to recall pictures from Romanian orphanages of children rejected from the moment of birth rocking endlessly to and fro in their filthy cots to know that this is so. Long before a child has language to put into words what she sees, she needs to witness daily demonstrations of loving commitment between the adults whose care of her body is essential for her survival. The adults' visible care of each other can do so much for the well-being of her developing soul. As soon as she can hear them, she needs to be told the stories of her conception and birth; its meaning and importance to parents, extended family and community.

So what kind of childhood did Jesus have, what kind of parenting did he receive? Demonstrative parenting would be my guess. Parenting that demonstrated to Jesus three important truths: first, that he, Jesus, was infinitely lovable and able to please just by being himself; second, that he was connected to a universe that is kind; and third, that he was known by a God who is good. These three gifts can help a soul to develop a compassionate understanding of what it means to be human, and give a sense of power within to effect change through service. With these assured, there would be no need for the manger occupant to know with John's certainty that he was the Logos, the Word of God incarnate for the salvation of many. Time enough for that discovery.

Sadly, while our three truths may be simple, they can be difficult to convey. No parents are perfect and perfectly loving at all times, and consequently no child ever born can know only unconditional acceptance. Indeed, too many go hungry for the truth about their own goodness. Our souls ache to do good, for this is a family trait we inherit from the Creator of us all, but the messages we receive are mixed and confusion can lead to despair. While we can see that the universe is awesome, we also experience it as unpredictable and danger-ous. Think of those splendid television documentaries of the natural world. Turning to one channel we gasp at the sight of never-before-seen creatures from the depths of the ocean. Then if we click to another channel we find ourselves shivering before views of massive destruction wreaked by earthquakes, winds and volcanic fires. Even faith in a good God is difficult to pass on to a child – especially if religion has presented us with a God who is very far from being wholly good, in stories of a vengeful dictator waiting to catch us out in sin, and ready enough to flood the entire world as a response.

Reflect for a moment on your own experiences of birth, infancy and childhood as you remember them or have had them reported to you. What words would you use to describe the welcome you received, and what did it demonstrate to you about yourself, God and the universe, either by accident or intentionally? One woman told me how her child was a very large and very hungry baby. Unfortunately, he was born in a time when the advice to new mums was to feed every four hours, regardless of birth-weight and the screams of the infant. His mother took this advice. The received wisdom also advised parents against lifting and cuddling in response to screams. Her baby cried all day, as well he might. A hungry baby does not know anything about four-hourly feeds. For a newborn, recently expelled from the womb where all needs were fully met before they were even felt, hunger brings fear, panic and a protest against certain annihilation – and usually sufficiently loudly to bring a caring adult running. But when no one comes to answer that cry, what message is conveyed to the infant about himself, the universe and its Creator?

And you; do you think of yourself as fundamentally good, known and understood by a good God, and situated in a universe that is rooting for you? I hope so. These three are like the good fairies in the tale of *Sleeping Beauty*. Always present with the princess, they celebrate her joys and stay alert to the dangers besetting her. And though they cannot turn away every bad or difficult situation, they can use their goodness to offset evil and bring something creative to any situation. In their company, Sleeping Beauty is kept safe from despair in a life that can often be difficult, with despair always an option. Demonstrative love, first experienced through parents and always evident in what we call God's providence, safeguards us on our journey from womb to individuated personhood. The journey – as all parents know who have watched their children make it – is a perilous one, so the need for such love is great.

When my own children were infants, I did a lot of cheerful singing, as I moved about the house from one room to another. I understood that a nine-month-old infant has no way of knowing, when that special person leaves the room, if he or she will ever return. So I tried to reassure my infant that

I was never far away. Mostly I would carry the child with me, keeping her in my sight as much as possible, giving lots of hugs and feeding on demand, demonstrating to her that the universe is not such a scary place after all. Accidents will happen, of course, and I have often wondered what my 11-month-old son made of the day when I inadvertently trapped four of his fingers in the bathroom door. It left me with a horror of door hinges, such that I feel sick whenever I see a child playing dangerously close to one. What impression did it leave on my son's mind? What message did it give him about life? Thankfully, acts of demonstrative love – hugs and bedtime stories for the very young, trust and increasing amounts of responsibility as we grow older – can overcome many accidents and inadequacies and help us survive the most distressing elements involved in becoming an individual soul. Cumulatively they reassure us that:

> Our soul is oned to God,
> and unchangeable goodness,
> and therefore
> between God and our soul
> there is neither wrath nor forgiveness
> because
> there is no between.
> Because of the beautiful oneing
> That was made by God
> Between the body and the soul.
> (Mother Julian of Norwich, quoted
> in Cousineau, 1995)

Your soul is 'oned' to God. How true does this feel for you? Perhaps not very true; it seems that most of us feel a certain distance between ourselves and our Creator. We have gathered all the sensations of our birth and childhood and joined them together into a story not of connecting love, but of separation. Something tells us we are not what we should be. We sense a distance between expectations of us and the reality of our everyday lives. And we suspect that God is as disappointed as we are, or as our parents seem to be. One woman describes the day she recognized that she had confused God with her rather busy father. Imagine her surprise when she discovered that God never has a bad day; never brushes her off with excuses about being too busy, or just popping off to play golf. Following fast on this insight came another, when a few days later she realized that what she wanted from God, even now as a grown woman, was favouritism rather than justice for all.

We need to see ourselves in relationship to God more clearly if we are to discover our true identity. God is not disappointed in any of us and has no favourites. Most of us will benefit from reflecting a little on our experience of childhood to sort out from our memories a few misapprehensions we developed there about life, God and ourselves.

Take some time to ponder some of the childhood memories you have, both joyful and sorrowful, and consider that God hopes for something good to come to you now from even the most painful of them. For:

Every moment and every event of every man's life on earth plant something in his soul. For just as the wind carries thousands of winged seeds, so each moment brings with it germs of spiritual vitality that come to rest imperceptibly in the minds and wills of men. (Merton, 1972)

We will find it helpful to pray for the grace to discover that our God is not (and never was) the God of disappointment, but instead of hope and spiritual vitality. Reading thoughtfully and prayerfully the letters, prayers and other writings of people who came to know Christ well – like Mother Julian, Teresa of Avila, Merton and Ignatius of Loyola – can help us with this grace. Discover this for yourself by using the poem about a soul that is 'oned' to God as a prayer. Substitute 'my soul' where appropriate until you can own something of the confidence and gratitude that Mother Julian herself felt as she wrote the words. God can replace your story of separation with a message of unchangeable goodness. But this will be a gradual replacement, so give it time.

Of course this sense of separation we all feel to varying degrees must have been a possibility for Jesus too unless his parents were perfect and living in a perfectly predictable world where fingers never get trapped in doors. Yet Jesus managed to grow into a most unusual person: one who not only felt 'oned' to God, but could say: 'To have seen me is to have seen the Father' (John 14.9). No separation there – how was this possible?

I imagine that like any mother Mary could remember with clarity the things that were said about her newborn son. The admiring, even wondering, words of those present at the birth; the goodwill, even reverence, of early visitors; the prophetic, even alarming, messages from the congregation. These were all significant to Mary.

All newborns command adoring attention, even worship. Few folk can gaze upon a baby without wanting to praise, without feeling reverent or even prophetic. This is as it should be since each new life is a new message of hope from God. When I was born the midwife took a look at my legs and declared, 'She's going to be a ballerina.' In much the same way, Simeon held the baby Jesus in his arms and said:

> Now, Master, you can let your servant go in peace, just
> as you promised; because my eyes have seen the salva-
> tion which you have prepared for all the nations to see,
> a light to enlighten the pagans and the glory of your
> people Israel. (Luke 2.29–32)

Then Simeon looked at the parents standing wonderingly
before him. What he says next makes me think that as he
blessed them, he suddenly felt the dead weight of an adult
man in his arms. To Mary he speaks:

> You see this child: he is destined for the fall and for the
> rising of many in Israel, destined to be a sign that is
> rejected – and a sword will pierce your own soul too –
> so that the secret thoughts of many may be laid bare.
> (Luke 2.34–5)

As it turned out, I did not become a ballerina. However, my
mother still remembers what the midwife said. Long ago
she passed it on to me. It is one of my birth narratives. It tells
me I received a welcome to the world and was offered a
meaningful future the very moment I was born. I am sure
something of this welcome communicated itself to my soul.

While still an infant Jesus would have listened to many of
his own birth narratives. No doubt Mary teased her son
about the inconvenience of his arrival at the dead of night
with nothing prepared and no chance of medical attention.
What fun she might have had regaling him with colourful
descriptions of exotic visitors from the east, and of shepherds
stumbling off the hills much the worse for drink and babbling
about angelic voices as they stood gawping in the doorway.
Family stories, personal stories, hilarious tales and absorbing
mysteries: we can imagine Jesus heard them all and, just as we

do with our birth narratives, accepted them as part of his story. They provided him with unforgettable clues to the unique event of his birth and its meaning for the world; a meaning that would spring not from his divinity but from his humanity.

Later he would have listened enthralled as Mary told other stories of God's way with his chosen people: stories of Abraham, Isaac, Jacob, Joseph, tales of stern prophets, of wise or foolish kings, of ingenious women and courageous men. Together these tales told of a God who reveals himself gradually through many interconnecting human stories. A God who discloses the divine will and intention bit by bit, so as not to overwhelm either mankind's freedom (including his freedom to doubt) or sanity.

Then as the boy grew, Joseph would have opened the Law to Jesus, teaching him all the precepts he would need to lead a blameless life before Yahweh. Teaching him too what was required of a good Jew, and what was wise, in a land occupied and ruled harshly by Rome. Attending the synagogue, sitting first with his mother behind the screen then with his father and the other men, Jesus would have listened as the Law was opened and its words of life read out loud by elders.

This is how life began for Jesus. Since his parents, family, friends and neighbours were not perfect and the political situation at the time of his childhood was far from idyllic, Jesus would at times have received other messages too: that he was separated from what he was meant to be. He was not a Roman citizen at a time when Rome's occupation stridently declared the inferiority of anything not part of that empire. Perhaps he was not a zealous hater of everything Roman either, as some of his playmates in Nazareth must surely have been, boasting of how they would join the guerrillas in the hills to help overthrow these oppressors. How Jesus interpreted the plethora of childhood messages and experiences would depend on how often each was communicated to him and by whom. It is the same for us, and for all of us there are three possible responses.

We may conclude, as many people seem to, that we are on our own in this life; that God is nowhere and existence merely an accident. This is indeed separation.

Or we may decide that God is an ingredient in life, a part of our story and, if we are religious, then a significant part. The soul is back in the body. And a belief arises among the majority of religious folk, including many Christians active in church and earnest in service, that God is ours to tell. The Creator of everything is a part of our text; a character in our tale. So we try to tell our story by fitting the God-character into the joys and sorrows of our experience and the facts of our situation and condition. 'God hates the sin and loves the sinner', those of us stuck on a tale of personal morality (since childhood) insist. In fact, God absorbs the one and redeems the other, understanding both. It is we in our ignorance and fear who hate both the sin and the sinner, and so we pray for God to fit in with our telling of the sin story. Such squeezing of God into our religious plot may help us cope with the difficult themes of life, but it has also led to the Church's lamentable history of violence in the past and seeming irrelevance in the present.

Ignatius encouraged people to find God in everything, but he also cautioned not to try and fit this personally communicating God into a life-story already full to overflowing with our plans and prejudices mapped out and lovingly poured over by our own egos. Any attempt to squeeze the infinite into a limited and congested fragment of life does not bring us closer to God, but reinforces a feeling of separation – sometimes even alienation – from our Creator. After all, human history in its entirety could never begin to accommodate the cosmic proportions of God's still unfolding drama.

Jesus did not respond to the messages of his childhood in either of these two ways. He did not reject or marginalize God. Instead, he took a third way. As he approached adolescence the desire he felt to do good in a way that would be unique to him made him as restless as every other teenager before and after him. He felt the need to embark on a personal quest for God, hoping to find a God who was busy creating a world that was intrinsically good. Because Joseph and Mary taught him well, and hugged him often.

And so, at the age of 12, he travelled to Jerusalem with his family and neighbours to celebrate the Feast of the Passover. After the great ceremonies and celebrations were over, and when the caravan of pilgrims had begun to wend its way back to Nazareth, Jesus disappeared. I can quite understand how Mary and Joseph went a whole day's journey without thinking anything of the fact that Jesus was not with them because my husband and I once took a 13-year-old nephew on holiday with us. We did a lot of walking on the holiday and always the nephew trailed reluctantly twenty metres or so behind us. He was protesting of course. Walking was boring, and walking with two adults particularly so. We paid him little attention, trusting him to catch us up when he felt like it. Mary and Joseph, it seems, just presumed that Jesus was somewhere in the company and would catch up with them when he was hungry. But no. Three days of increasingly frantic searching and questioning by Mary and Joseph followed, but revealed nothing. Then they heard word of a young boy causing a stir in the Temple courtyards and finally caught sight of Jesus debating passionately with the elders about the meaning of Scripture and its interpretation by the Law.

Jesus, with the aplomb of any adolescent who has just given his parents a heart-stopping fright, asks casually, '[Did you not know] I must be about my Father's business?' (Luke 2.49, AV). His surprise, though no comfort to his demented parents, is understandable. It seems that Jesus had, like his mother before him, experienced some kind of illumination, a moment of clarity and insight that might well shape the course of his life, though it would not insist on this. The boy in him expects his parents to read his mind and follow his logic, without him having to communicate either of these to them. What was impossible for them is possible for us because we know the rest of the story. So what was the nature of this insight Jesus belatedly tries to share with his parents?

The verse in Luke 2.49 is translated in many different ways, but the core of meaning certainly seems to be: Did you not know I must always be where my Father is. It is a word about the religious experience and identity of Jesus which Mary and Joseph, and Jesus too, had to receive at that moment. This word of truth and identity must have come to them like a two-edged sword which revealed not only Jesus' identity, but also the identity of Mary and Joseph in relationship to Him. Perhaps Mary had to confront for the first time the reality that, though she was mother, her son did not in some real way belong to her. More accurately, perhaps, she had to ponder newly *how* he belonged to her (for, ultimately, the more He is from and for His Father the more entirely is He hers – and ours). One wonders also whether Jesus himself did not have to ponder deeply the word of truth and identity that had been *given* to Him there in His Father's house. (Fleming, 1983)

It might be useful to ponder what it means for you to belong to your parents and in what ways any children you have belong to you. Jesus' story teaches us that a person who discovers his or her own identity in God can become even more to their parents than a son or daughter; more to their friends than a friend; more to their partner than a loved other. This happens because as we become our true selves we also become more fully a part of what God has in mind for creation. So when we meet and interact with others, God's salvation meets them too. Jesus was more than Mary's and Joseph's son; he was their redeemer. I am more than a sister to my brother; I am the keeper of his soul; his saviour. Or at least I will be, and he mine, when we begin to live the truth of our own souls. We are intimately and existentially connected to each other no matter how inconvenient that seems at times.

And at times it seems very inconvenient. When we are busy oppressing whole continents of our brothers and sisters with our economic policies, or bombing a country full of their homes, it is awkward to be reminded that these people are intimately connected to us. But the gospel tells us that what we do to the least of these, we do to Christ and – through Christ – to ourselves. Closer to home, and in the rough and tumble of human relationships, it can be awkward to be reminded that this other from whom I want something – a job or some kind of affirmation, or perhaps a return of the passionate love I am offering – is connected to me in a way that takes priority over any of these.

The greatest priority we all should have, according to Jesus, is to love that other person as though he/she were me. That means I want for this other what I want for.myself. What I want for myself is the freedom to be who I am in my soul. Do I really desire this for everyone I meet? What I

35

really want I will be prepared to work to bring about with my actions, my words and my prayers. So pray for God to change the world into a community of free and lively souls who are 'one in Christ Jesus'(Galatians 3.28); and pray for this redemption to begin with you.

Perhaps it already has. Many of us can point to an experience in childhood or adolescence that, in retrospect, was the beginning of our conscious and personal awareness of God's interest in us. People describe a numinous experience that has kept its flavour over many years or they speak of a defining moment, but often it is one that neither compelled much notice at the time nor insisted on its own veracity. It is just as likely to have been an experience easily overlooked and, with the passage of time, packed away with childhood toys.

I remember walking home from school one day at the age of 13. I had said goodbye to my friends as one by one they turned off from the main road. Now I walked on alone, my house still some way distant. I remember that the road traffic was noisy beside me, but I have no recollection of my thoughts except that from somewhere there arose in me the realization that God *was*. It was nothing more than a strong hunch, but I remember thinking that it was a hunch that held huge implications for my future life.

Perhaps you too have a memory of a defining moment in your life. It need not be a particularly religious experience, such as the one Jesus had in the Temple. It might be a day when you sensed God's presence and interest in your life, or it could be a day when you knew you had to be a teacher, actor, doctor, etc. Take some time to allow any memories to surface. Don't be concerned if nothing comes to mind. It could be that you are looking too hard. Trust that God is capable of working in the background to bring to your conscious memory the incident if it exists. Allow a couple of days for this. Don't be surprised if a useful memory pops into your head just before you fall asleep or when you are relaxing in the bath.

But even if no memory comes to mind, don't worry; it is helpful rather than essential. Some of us have defining moments and can recall them, some have good childhoods, some have many gifts, some have many sorrows. Some of us experience certain things in life, but none of us experiences everything. Nor is it necessary that we do – not if separation from all that sustains and gives meaning to life and identity is only a misapprehension; not if we are 'oned' to God and, through God, to one another. The gospel message is that *together* we can experience the fullness of life that God has in mind for us.

It is a message put into practice by one teacher I know. She has a time set aside once a week or so for what she calls 'the sharing circle'. The children are invited to leave their work and gather in a circle on the floor. They then share that week's stories with one another. One child has had a birthday and tells of the exciting presents received. Others recall their own birthdays and re-live the happiness. Another has had a trip to the orthodontist and shows off his new braces, explaining how uncomfortable they feel. Everyone sympathizes; every child has or knows of a story about the horrors of dentistry. Then perhaps there has been trouble in the playground; a quarrel has broken out between chums. Here is the place to explore the difficulties and the pain. Children not involved will offer advice; sometimes tears are shed. Better ways are sought and found for dealing with life's ups and downs. Empathy is nurtured in this circle and an important truth demonstrated: sharing our stories allows the experience of one to become the experience of all. The children return to their desks feeling empowered to do good. Having been affirmed by their teacher and friends, they sense themselves as connected to something bigger, a kindly universe. And, of course, so they are.

Remembering not just our own stories, but hearing also those of our family and ancestors, our neighbours and friends and their ancestors, is powerful, putting us in touch with the corpus of lived experience and the context for our future hope. If we put all our stories together as John put together the stories and reports about his friend Jesus, we too will come up with the gospel: good news about the meaning and purpose of life.

And whether or not we have our own defining moment of illumination and clarity we can all reflect on this moment in Jesus' life and ask ourselves: why should we be surprised when one among us chooses to be about the business of becoming intimately connected to God? Thomas Merton wrote: 'God utters me like a word containing a partial thought of Himself' (Merton, 1972). I think Jesus felt this too, and from an early age. Whether or not the same is true of us, it is never too late to discover that divine thought we are asked to express with our lives. And since Love never gives up, and even the oldest among us still has all the potential of a 12-year-old in the eyes of God, we can still learn from what we presently live. As we take time to contemplate this story of the boy Jesus and his parents (who perhaps had come to believe that God was, after all, just a part of their story), it can still proclaim those three important truths to us. We are infinitely lovable. We are and always will be connected to a universe that is kind. We are intimately known and understood by a God who is good. This being so, we too are called to the important business that occupies our Father.

References

Cousineau, P. (ed.), *Soul: An Archaeology*. London, Thorsons, 1995.

Fleming, SJ, David L. (ed.), 'Notes on the Spiritual Exercises of St Ignatius of Loyola', in *Review for Religious*. St Louis, 1983.

Merton, Thomas, *Seeds of Contemplation*. Wheathampstead, Anthony Clarke Books, 1972.

Peterson, Eugene, *The Message*. Colorado, NavPress Publishing Group, 1993.

4

First Principles

I wonder if there are twenty men alive in the world now who see things as they really are. That would mean there were twenty men who were free, who were not dominated or even influenced by any attachment to any created thing or to their own selves or to any gift of God, even to the highest, the most supernaturally pure of His graces. I don't believe that there are twenty such men alive in the world. But there must be one or two. They are the ones who are holding everything together and keeping the universe from falling apart.

(Merton, 1972)

Jesus spent the next eighteen or so years doing ordinary things while his faith grew in a God personally interested in and intimately connected to him. He worked and played, ate and slept, and carried out countless insignificant tasks in those hidden years. He may not always have felt that same clarity he experienced in the Temple. Often he may have doubted that his very ordinary life as a carpenter in Nazareth could accomplish anything for the Father. What is true for Jesus is true for us. We too are employed in the family business, but we do not always sense this. Often we cannot see how our faith is making a difference to our world. Our days are ordinary ones filled with mundane tasks, little joys and sorrows, many wasted moments. We rarely if ever feel the presence of God as we worship or pray. These are the hidden years of our faith, but God is at work in them fashioning an intimate connection between him and us, just as he did in those quiet years of Jesus' life.

Then the time came for Nazareth to deliver Jesus from her womb as Mary had done 30 years before. The waters broke with the news of John preaching at the River Jordan, triggering in Jesus a sense that it was time to go; to be always where the Father is. What drew him away from his life as a carpenter in Nazareth and what allowed him to go? Surely it was that rare freedom that Thomas Merton describes.

Rare because though most of us want to know who we are, why we are here, and what path in life will bring us happiness by the time we reach adulthood we want other things too. While the idea of a purposeful and fulfilling life where we know, love, and serve God may be attractive, other things attract us even more. Sometimes we can be so stuck on a person, a job, an idea, that we feel we simply cannot live without them. We may sense God inviting us to work out our own salvation, but we would like to negotiate the terms of the deal. There are a few things we are reluctant to let go of; familiar and comforting aspects of our routine that we no longer can envisage doing without.

We live in a society able and willing to offer us, at a price, all kinds of substitutes for authentic freedom. These things all too easily obscure that one simple truth every saint in heaven knows, and that Ignatius explains explicitly: substance abuse is bad for the soul. Here is what he says about it in what he calls the First Principle and Foundation of his Spiritual Exercises:

God freely created us so that we might know, love and

ı in this life and be happy with him forever.
ɹrpose in creating us is to draw forth from us a
se of love and service here on earth, so that we
ɪttain our goal of everlasting happiness with him in
heaven. All the things in this world are gifts of God,
created for us, to be the means by which we can come
to know him better, love him more surely, and serve him
more faithfully. As a result, we ought to appreciate and
use these gifts of God insofar as they help us toward our
goal of loving service and union with God. But insofar
as any created things hinder our progress toward our
goal, we ought to let them go. (Fleming, 1978)

We all know good sense when we read it, but sometimes we
forget that *everything* created by God is a 'substance' we can
either enjoy or misuse. When I am inordinately attached to a
created thing such that I cannot conceive of living with less
or none of it, I give that created thing power over me. 'If
music be the food of love, play on that having surfeit of it
the appetite may sicken and so die' (*Twelfth Night*) – so sighed
Orsinò, made powerless by his unrequited love of the Countess
Olivia. Unfortunately, our appetite for some things never
sickens, nor dies. Rather it feeds on itself, leaving us no better
off than a heroin addict, even supposing our addiction is to
the most supernaturally pure grace Merton has in mind.
Any powerful addiction interferes with my connection to
you and every other good creation of God's. It interferes with
the connection between myself and God, making me dis-
eased in my soul. To be truly who I am requires that I be
wholly available to God's choices for me. After all, God is the
artist and I the material.

Addiction to the status quo or to any created thing, including
an idea, severely restricts my availability to God. If I am hooked
on success in my career, I am hardly likely to be available to

a God who is quietly insisting that a more meaningful life is to be found in a more modest endeavour. If I am besotted by the idea of personal morality, I may never recognize that I am afraid to believe in a wholly good and unconditionally loving God. If I am fiercely independent, striving for my own self-actualization, it will be hard to turn aside or slow my pace and join the community venture of wholeness and holiness that God is labouring over with infinite patience and skill. Addictive behaviour, even of the most pious or religious kind, squeezes out other people and impoverishes me to the point where I, like the lawyer in Luke's Gospel, have to be reminded, 'Who is my neighbour?' (Luke 10.29).

Now most of us are addicts to some extent or other. For those of us who desire wholeness and holiness, a radical and step-by-step reordering of life both material and spiritual is called for. The psychotherapist Scott Peck calls this reordering *kenosis*: 'the process of the self emptying itself of self' (Peck, 1997), or of 'the ego bumping itself off', so that God's will can hold sway in a person's life.

In his letter to the church at Philippi, Paul urges the people there to follow the example of *kenosis* that we see in Christ Jesus:

> His state was divine,
> yet he did not cling
> to his equality with God
> but emptied himself
> to assume the condition of a slave,
> and became as men are;
> and being as all men are,
> he was humbler yet,
> even to accepting death,
> death on a cross.
>
> (Philippians 2.6–8)

As he left Nazareth and all that was dear to him about his life there, Jesus emptied himself to become totally available to God with no rights at all, not even the right to life itself. And just in case we are foolish enough to underestimate either the importance or the difficulty of his and our *kenosis*, Scott Peck issues a warning:

> But make no mistake *kenosis* does not come easily or naturally. I am virtually certain that I myself could not follow a *kenotic* path, accepting without denial the stripping away of illusions and competencies that death and dying demand, nor could I welcome this stripping, were it not for my spiritual belief system. I couldn't do it unless I believed in a God who wanted me stripped away so that She could have me totally naked without any of the deceptive clothing of my ego . . . unless I had a personal relationship with God so that, among other things, I could complain to Him about His violence and possessiveness . . . unless I was convinced that I had a soul whose highest destiny was utterly and voluntarily to belong to Him . . . unless I knew with certainty that my only true power resided in my soul, that every effective and healing accomplishment of mine had been Her accomplishment emanating out of my real being, my soul, which She created, and that every stupid and wicked thing I have done originated in my ego and its self-preservative mechanisms . . . and unless I realized my ego to be but a temporary necessity, that it chose to cooperate with God as best it could and that I was forgiven from the day of my birth. (Peck, 1997)

This is a passage that sends a shiver down my spine. If it has a similar impact on you, it is probably because some part of you recognizes and longs for *kenosis*. Allow this thought to sink in; it is an important insight and one for which you can feel grateful. Spend time slowly reading and re-reading Peck's description of *kenosis*, stopping to savour or ponder any phrase that seems either to comfort or discomfort you. Taking heed of Peck's observation that *kenosis* is impossible without God's help, pray for a deep awareness of the radical consequences that any reordering of your life and faith is likely to involve. Over the next two or three days, whenever you remember, ask God for a deep desire for *kenosis*, and an understanding of what it means for you personally. This desire, with understanding that you can only pray for and not work yourself into, is itself a sign. A sign reassures us that we are on the right road; that God does indeed long to free us from the clutter of life and for the discovery of our own true and unrepeatable identity and meaning.

To assist your reflections, spend time listing all the created gifts (including people) in your life that seem to encourage your availability to God. Next list all the created gifts (again including people) in your life at present that hinder this. But remember that God is not your conscience, and note that personality is not the sum total of the self. Let us say, for example, that you vaguely feel that your habit of dropping into the pub on the way home from work might somehow be reducing your availability to God. This may indeed be so, yet God is not going ape over your weekly alcohol consumption. Common sense will tell you if change is needed for the good of your health, but *kenosis* is more likely to point to any unease in your life that lurks unidentified and powerful behind the pub habit. Similarly, you may assume that your weekly attendance at church makes you available to God when actually it only gives you a warm feeling inside of doing something that would have pleased your mother. Resist the temptation to be satisfied with either a guilt-list or a wish-list. Instead, pray for a deep understanding of the true (and often hidden) significance of each created thing in your life, and keep praying for the desire to be completely available to God.

Honest and open reflection will no doubt bring some surprises – especially if you can remember to think of yourself as both an individual and part of a community. Give thanks for each surprise. Your list of created things will gradually grow to contain both personal possessions (like a musical talent) and those possessions you enjoy as part of a privileged group. For example, democracy is an idea – and therefore a created gift that affects the lives of millions of people who live in democratic societies. But it also affects those who do not: people whose ordinary lives are touched by the foreign policies of powers like the United States of America. Are we better neighbours because of our attachment to the benefits of a democratic society or are we just more selective (like the priest and the Levite in the Good Samaritan story) about whose cries for justice and mercy we hear and respond to? For democracy can lead us towards God or away from God. It leads us towards God when it encourages us to treat others as we would have them treat us, both in our local setting and in national and international affairs. It leads us away from God whenever it suggests that a good end (such as the spread of democracy) justifies the means. According to the gospel of Jesus, this can never be true.

We saw in the previous chapter how John started his Gospel with a statement about who he believed Jesus to be. Similarly, Ignatius placed his First Principle and Foundation at the start of his book. It is not only his beginning point for a life of meaning, but also his destination; a premise and a promise, the means to an end and the end itself. Like any experienced pilgrim, both John and Ignatius understood the importance of knowing where one is headed before starting out on a journey. Praise, reverence and service of God – this is where Ignatius was headed and where he sought to draw others. He knew that when we offer praise, reverence and service to God we are truly ourselves, and that only when we discover and live our true selves will we be able to offer our unique and soul-felt praise, reverence and service to God. We too sense this. The idea of *kenosis* sends a thrill through us, not just because we all recognize a need to reorder our lives, bump off our egos, but because we all have a vision of how good life could be if we did.

So take some more time (noticing as you do that allowing yourself time for honest reflection leading into prayer is probably part of the reordering process) and use it to compose your own First Principle and Foundation. It should be a statement about the purpose of life formed from both your positive experience so far and the hope you have for the future. Do not worry at this point if what you write seems grandiose or reads like a fairy-tale. It is quite normal for us to have some illusions about our self and the life we are invited to live. Among the disordered illusions and attractive fantasies we all harbour lies the simple truth about who we are and what our lives could be. What is not true will become apparent through persistence in honest reflection and prayer.

Ignatius had fantasies too. The age we live in is often referred to as the 'postmodern age'; a stage in humanity's development when the grand narrative has lost its efficacy as social adhesive and personal signpost. St Ignatius was not a postmodern soul. He lived in a time of very grand narratives written by men, and for men, and filled with heroes doing famous deeds in battle and romantic deeds at court. Christopher Columbus was one such hero, discovering the New World and bringing home shiploads of treasure to the sumptuous palaces of already powerful Spanish monarchs. Within this milieu, and in spite of his own dreams of great chivalric deeds, Ignatius discovered that there is more to life, not less, than the grandest of man's narratives. Ignatius found that life, though it can be unremittingly hard, also has meaning, purpose and intention behind it, and that these are discoverable by us. We, however, seem to have thrown the baby out with the none-too-clean bath water of previous ages as this description of the postmodern soul by American author Sam Keen suggests:

> He is a blank page, a *tabula rasa*, upon which the moment writes its tale. Weightless, he suffers, in the words of Milan Kundera, 'the unbearable lightness of being.' Unlike the classical 'hero with a thousand faces,' he avoids the depths and keeps himself satiated with a thousand amusing façades. The mall, the automobile showroom, and the electronic supermarket are his catharsis. If he turns to more 'serious' matters he becomes what Trungpa Rinpoche called a 'spiritual materialist.' He samples religions and salvation schemes. (From *Fire in the Belly*, quoted in Cousineau, 1995)

This is a passage full of phrases to take with you through a day. Notice in yourself and those around you, friends and strangers, that 'unbearable lightness of being'. Try to spot where you avoid the depths. Identify some of the amusing façades you turn to for catharsis and in what ways you choose to 'sample religions and salvation schemes'. It is worth considering the plethora of religions available for sampling: career, family, sport, personal development, worship of youthfulness, reliance on crystals, to name but a few. Consider what the more serious matters of your life are and what space they are accorded both in your daily routine and your life orientation.

Finally, try all these exercises again while imagining what Jesus would have made of them. This may seem a strange idea, but I think you will be surprised how valuable it can be to take on the mind of Christ; to try and figure out his responses to life. So begin by trying to list the kind of created things that Jesus might have enjoyed, and that would have built upon his childhood experience of a good God creating a kind universe full of unique and irreplaceable souls.

Life in first-century Palestine clearly was very different from our own, but some things never change and the very best things in life are always around us: nature, art and music, relationships. It might be more difficult (and even more valuable!) to list some created things that could have drawn Jesus away from God or kept him in Nazareth. Once again, the difficulty lies with a misconception we have. We think that God's Son would necessarily be always perfectly focused on God. But Jesus was God's Son incarnate. For me this means he was a man with the same opportunities to discover God as we have – and the same potential for being drawn away from God as we have. We all know that even a child raised in a religious home by hard-working and sensible parents can choose not to embrace a living faith. Think of people you know who, with every advantage, are nevertheless being drawn away from what is good in life to what is expedient or available. Or think of charismatic religious leaders whose very zeal makes them impatient with God's careful labouring and drives them to re-create the world in the miniature form of a cult. If you are still having trouble deciding what created things had the potential to draw Jesus away from God, read the story of his temptation in the desert (Mark 1). We will look at this passage again in the next chapter, but it may help you with this present exercise.

Next compose for Jesus a First Principle and Foundation. Use the insights we pondered in Chapter 3, along with any others that occur to you, in order to summarize his positive experience and future hope. Remember that this statement is more than wishful thinking. It is a manifesto for the rest of his life, and a compass that, in the most extreme of situations, must point him in the direction of God. I think if you manage to catch anything of the soul of Christ in your attempt, what you write will send a thrill through you as you read it aloud.

Finally, re-read Sam Keen's description of the postmodern soul with Jesus in mind. What a contrast this is to the manifesto you have just written for him! Try to imagine the Jesus of the gospel being content with any of a thousand amusing façades. Try to recall one story of him avoiding the depths of what his life was about. Impossible, isn't it? He was too committed to his humanity to be satisfied with less than fullness of life for himself and for others.

When news of John the Baptizer reached him, Jesus could not ignore the sense he had that John was connected to his own search for identity in God. He could not quieten, with work or play or any distraction, the desire growing in him to go and see this man for himself. Jesus left Nazareth because he was free to follow his irresistible hunch that life in all its fullness waited for him in the waters of the Jordan.

References

Cousineau, P. (ed.), *Soul: An Archaeology*. London, Thorsons, 1995.

Fleming, SJ, David L., *Draw Me Into Your Friendship: The Spiritual Exercises. A Literal Translation and a Contemporary Reading*. St Louis, The Institute of Jesuit Sources, 1996.

Merton, Thomas, *Seeds of Contemplation*. Wheathampstead, Anthony Clarke Books, 1972.

Peck, M. Scott, *Denial of the Soul*. London, Simon & Schuster, 1997.

5

A Retreat in the Desert

Watch closely: I'm sending my preacher ahead of you;
He'll make the road smooth for you.
Thunder in the desert!
Prepare for God's arrival!
Make the road smooth and straight!
(Mark 1.1, Peterson, 1993)

Others in the village had gone to see this baptizing preacher and come back again. But something made Jesus prepare for a longer stay away. He spoke to family and friends, handed over the business and closed the door on the carpenter's shop watched by his mother. Mary, remembering the 12-year-old boy so confident of being about his Father's business, would have prayed silently (as was her way) for the man standing before her now fingering the wooden door uncertainly. What was her prayer at that moment or, rather, what prayer would you have offered in her place? Perhaps that Jesus would always know he had a home to return to, and that he would never feel tied to that home and its occupants. Roots and wings are the only gifts we can give our children. Of course, Mary knew what Jesus vaguely sensed at this moment: that John, who had recognized God's son in the womb, would surely recognize him in the man. The time had come for Jesus to discover his true identity in God and Mary was glad for him. But still she could feel the sword of anxiety piercing her side as she watched him walk away from her.

He heard the crowds at the river before he saw them. Hundreds milling around, talking, laughing, crying. He asked for John and they pointed. In the middle of the water stood a man. Tenderly, he was helping an old woman up off her knees. Stroking the hair that clung to her head and dripped down her back, he spoke softly to her. They hugged, and then two men standing close came forward to help the woman from the river and usher another to take her place. An hour passed before Jesus stood in front of John.

It was to be an important encounter. 'You are my Son, the Beloved; my favour rests on you' (Mark 1.11) God declared, and both men heard it. No wonder Jesus took himself off to the desert. He had a lot to think about. So do we. We are all sons and daughters of God. All beloved. God is proud of each one of us. Offers each of us roots and wings so that we can soar to the heights of our human potential while finding our home in the depths of a Father's love. What might we become if we allow this freedom to animate our lives? And what other messages about ourselves will we need to disregard in the process? These are the questions that Jesus took with him on his desert retreat.

If you have ever managed to go away from home for a few days of quiet prayer (and I recommend the experience!), you will know that a lot can happen in a very short space of time. Usually at the beginning of a retreat it is important to spend some time relaxing, catching up on sleep, letting the body tell us what it needs in the way of food, exercise, rest and recreation. We may find ourselves falling asleep even during the times we have set aside for prayer. Nevertheless, what prayer we manage is often delightfully easy and rich, full of images and insights. God seems close; generously nurturing our faith, hope and love. We too hear those reassuring words: 'You are my Son, the Beloved' (Mark 1.11) and we respond with a resolve to live as a person who trusts in this loving Father.

Then somewhere around the middle of the retreat things have a way of changing. The prayer dries up or becomes very distracted. We may begin to wonder why we are here when there are so many things we could more usefully be doing at home. The insights of a day ago seem foolish or banal. The decisions we made – that God is good and can be trusted, that we are loved and lovable, that life invites a response of energy and commitment from us – all these suddenly need to be revisited. We tell our retreat director something of this and she nods encouragingly as though the news were good. Here is why: whenever we resolve to pay more attention to our soul than to a thousand amusing façades, we can expect to meet some resistance within. What we are experiencing, though not as jolly or as comfortable as the earlier prayer, is an important indication that our prayer is deepening. If this were not so, there would be no necessity for our resistance to wake up and start making its presence felt.

In fact, very often the resistance begins even before we commit ourselves to this prayerful listening. Some of us, though we hear God's words of approval each week as we worship in church, put off indefinitely the discovery of our own identity. We are afraid to let that approval do more than comfort us fleetingly before we put our heads down for the next week of meaningless grind. If we pay closer attention to what God is saying about us, too much may be asked of us and too few of our present attachments prove necessary. We are not ready to place ourselves in the hands of the God that

Peck (1997) describes as wanting 'me stripped away so that She could have me totally naked without any of the deceptive clothing of my ego . . .' Perhaps we know that we lack the kind of relationship with God that would allow us to 'complain to Him about His violence and possessiveness . . .' Or perhaps we just remain unconvinced that we have 'a soul whose highest destiny was utterly and voluntarily to belong to Him . . .' and so we prevaricate while God's dream waits a little longer to be realized.

It is also possible, whether or not we go away on retreat, to begin the labour of listening only to change our minds about the necessity for this a little way down the road of prayer. Changing our resolve is something people do all the time of course. Usually it is New Year's Eve when we make a decision for the coming year: a resolution regarding some area of our life. We will stop smoking, or get more exercise, start a new hobby, or take control of our finances. We know we will be happier within ourselves through the keeping of this resolution. But our resolution is not an easy thing, and so a few days later, with our resolve melted away and discomfort all around, we begin the process of changing our minds. January is never a good month to go on a diet, we tell ourselves, better to wait until the spring. Giving up cigarettes is of course the only sensible option, but the stress it places me under is surely doing as much damage to my health – and certainly to my happiness. With barely a sigh of regret, we light up that cigarette or reach for the chocolate biscuits. Something very similar can happen to our prayer.

A person who has resolved to pay close attention, perhaps with the help of a spiritual director, to God's communication to them will inevitably be inclined sooner rather than later to stop. Usually the whole endeavour begins to appear too difficult or too self-absorbed, or just irrelevant to the world's

54

needs. Sometimes the person's early enthusiasm is choked by the messages given in childhood that he or she is too wicked or weak to be of any significance or interest to God at all.

None of these things are true, but they can feel true and they can stop us in our tracks. In our confusion God appears disappointed or distant or we feel ourselves beyond the pale. Faith in the goodness of God, hope for a purposeful future or love for ourselves and others, is difficult. When this happens, and it happens to all of us regularly, there is no need to panic – and in fact every reason to be encouraged.

After all, Jesus had a similar experience on his desert retreat. At first God was close, generous with insights and nurturing of faith, hope and love. Jesus was encouraged to trust his baptismal experience. Then something changed, and Jesus inclined his ear towards other voices. They suggested most reasonably that his restless hunch could be wrong. After all, he was only 12 years old when he first became aware of the still small voice of God calling him to a unique and unrepeatable life. What does a 12-year-old know? Yes, he had heard the same promise at the River Jordan, but it did not get any easier to believe in spite of years of prayer and religious experience. He was a carpenter, a good and honest craftsman devout in religious observance and careful in familial responsibilities. Is it likely that God would ask more of him?

And so Jesus faced temptation in the middle of his desert retreat. Perhaps he was wrong. And even if he was right, he saw all too clearly how dangerous things could become if he dared to listen to his insistent soul. The religious leaders would feel threatened by someone with no sense of separation between himself and God. The Roman occupation would grow nervous around a man who had no need of personal dignity, whose understanding of wealth and freedom were so different from theirs as to be revolutionary. Ordinary people would cry for blood if he suggested that they relinquish their dream of victory over Roman invaders and look instead for God's intention in the here-and-now reality of their lives as an occupied nation.

There must be another interpretation to be placed on all of this. And of course several other interpretations came easily to his mind. Perhaps God meant him to use his gifts simply to fulfil a personal need for meaning and purpose by living quietly as a private citizen. No need to challenge anyone with his crazy dream if he was content to turn stones into bread enough to satisfy his own hunger. But then man cannot truly live on bread and alone, can he?

Alternatively, he could strive for public honour, power and riches. With a bit of effort and the help of his charismatic personality, the glory of every kingdom ever known to man might be his. Once he had the power he could use it to make a difference in the lives of so many who cried out for justice. But then what would it profit him to gain the whole world in this way if it meant losing his own irreplaceable soul?

Easiest of all was to call God's bluff on this crazy dream he was dreaming. He would throw himself off this high point. If God was really interested in him, the divine hand would have to show itself by saving him from death on the rocks of conformity far below. But then despair like this was just a subtle way of putting God to the test, wasn't it?

On his desert retreat Jesus seriously thought about changing his mind. He was tempted to settle for what was expedient in life, to plunge into acceptable conformity, and give up his dream of having a unique, a once-in-a-universe, vocation. The fact that he refused these alternatives does not mean that they held no real and lasting attraction for him, but the thought of them gave him no peace and failed to lift his spirits from a certain confusion he was presently experiencing. Better to stick with his previous decision for the moment. If what he felt God had in mind for him was wrong, then that would become apparent and later, when he was feeling more hopeful than at present, he could review the situation.

Holding fast is not the easy option. Even after years of regular prayer and reflection with many insights into the kindness of God and the providence of his/her world, a person will hit times of spiritual discouragement. These come and go rather like clouds in the sky do, but when we are sitting under a particularly dark cloud it can seem as though it will never shift. So we remake our plans to help us cope with this changed condition, forgetting that in a little while the cloud will move away again and everything will look and feel different. In a time of discouragement, or what Ignatius calls spiritual desolation, we can be tempted to discard all that we learned and trusted in a previous and more encouraging period about our self and our life in God.

So it was for Joan, a woman who took two years of disciplined prayer and honest reflection to complete the Spiritual Exercises. By profession a nurse, Joan also suffered from ME and needed to pay close attention to her body, mind and spirit to avoid doing too much and throwing herself into a debilitating relapse. During the retreat it began to emerge that Joan's enormous sense of responsibility for the welfare of those around her went far beyond what God asked of her. Over the years (and this began in childhood) it had become something that possessed her and, though it looked holy and good, was actually destroying her health and happiness. She was like Jesus on the pinnacle of the Temple when he was inclined to throw himself off, daring God to save him. Joan was being tempted to disregard her own safety, to throw herself recklessly at every situation of need that she encountered, compelling God to make sure she did not smash into a thousand pieces. God wanted Joan to know that he/she cared for her too. It was not God's will that she make herself ill through making others better.

Now the gospel tells us that after Jesus' retreat in the desert, the tempter withdrew with the clear intention of returning to confuse and misguide him another time. The way this works for us is simple. The clarity of an insight like the one Joan received, though it initially brings a sense of gratitude and hope for the future, begins to diminish over time. We need to keep it before us in prayer, asking for the grace of an ever-deeper awareness and understanding of its importance for our freedom. But often we neglect to do this. We are like the person Paul talked of who looks in a mirror, sees the true reflection there and then turns away, forgetting what he saw.

Some months after completing the Spiritual Exercises Joan's temptation to exhaust herself completely reappeared, looking (as it always did) like the only thing a good person could do in very demanding family circumstances. Fortunately, she was sufficiently aware to pause before plunging off the precipice, choosing instead to talk things over with her spiritual director.

Take a moment or two to recall a time when the news was better than you could have dreamed possible. Perhaps your exam grades were a pleasant surprise, or a job interview secured you the job when you thought you had blown it. Perhaps an illness in the family was less serious than first thought, or you discovered that God was not as hung up on something in your life that felt to you like a major difficulty. Joan's good news was that God wanted her to look after herself. Remember just how delighted you felt, and grateful and enlivened by your news, and remember the plans you made out of your new hope or faith in yourself or in life or

God. Once you have remembered and can feel again the consolation you enjoyed at that time, ask yourself what happened next. Was this a transient thing, or did it become a consolation that continued to nurture your faith and inform your choices?

We can learn to distinguish between a time of consolation in prayer when faith, hope and love are real and we feel drawn to God in everything we see, and times of desolation when we feel confused or less sure of God than previously. Then it becomes possible to recognize temptation each time it makes an appearance in our lives. A golden rule of Ignatius is to hold fast in a time of desolation to the decision we made in a previous time of consolation. This is what Jesus did and what Joan learned to do. Sometimes holding fast is all that is needed to blow away that cloud of desolation and deal with a temptation. However, Ignatius gives some advice for what else can prove helpful:

> We can become discerning persons by examining carefully our own experiences. If in reflecting on the course of our thoughts or our actions we find that from the beginning to end our eyes have remained fixed on the Lord, we can be sure that the good spirit has been moving us. But if what started off well in our thought and action begins to be self-focussed or to turn us from our way to God, we should suspect that the evil spirit has somehow twisted the good beginning to an evil direction, and possibly even to an evil end. So we can discover that an original good course has led us to be weakened spiritually or even to become desolate or confused. The signs of desolation give clear indication of the evil spirit's influence.

When we recognise that we have been duped by the

evil spirit through a certain thought progression or course of action, we should review carefully all the stages which we passed through from the time when the evil became apparent back to its very beginnings in the good. By means of such a review, we will find that we can more quickly catch ourselves when we are being led on by the deceit of the evil spirit and so we are more enabled to guard ourselves in the future. (Fleming, 1978)

You may find the language old-fashioned in the light of modern psychology, but don't be tempted to overlook the wisdom of this passage regarding the usefulness of discernment. Not every thought, feeling and inclination I experience is pointing me in the direction of God's will for me, because though I am attracted to a life intimately connected to God, part of me is inclined to resist this attraction. So my soul has an enemy and I need to recognize the movement of that enemy within me.

Discernment is simply the ability to notice, accept and work with the truth that when I go to pray, very often I am not alone. I am like the Gerasene demoniac who ran to meet Jesus, his mind fragmented by thousands of conflicting influences and passions. My name is Legion. There are thousands of us. When I pray I am accompanied by all my images of God, the cosy, the frightening, the false and the authentic. My passions are there too, all crying out to be heard; I want God, but I want a rich prayer time, full of images and insights. I want God, but I want success. I want God, but I want security. I want God, but I want approval or popularity. The messages I have received in childhood about myself, the world and its Creator are all there too, telling me what I may become and what I may as well give up hope of ever becoming. Making sense of all of this will take energetic prayer for the graces that only God can give. This requires that I become not just a person who prays, but a person who prays with discernment.

Jesus was led by the Spirit into the desert so that he might become a discerning person, able to spot his enemy and mine in every invitation to abandon his dream for a life of respectable conformity. When he walked back out of the desert he still had more to learn. Discerning the voice of God from among all the other messages we receive is an ongoing daily task – one for which the twenty-third psalm might well have been written. In the next chapter we will look at what help the psalmist offered Jesus, and can offer us as we seek to hold fast to God's decision about our inestimable worth and unique identity.

References

Fleming, SJ, David L., *Draw Me Into Your Friendship: The Spiritual Exercises. A Literal Translation and a Contemporary Reading*. St Louis, Institute of Jesuit Sources, 1996.

Peck, M. Scott, *Denial of the Soul*. London, Simon & Schuster, 1997.

Peterson, Eugene, *The Message*. Colorado, NavPress Publishing Group, 1993.

6

Paths of Virtue

Yahweh is my shepherd,
  I lack nothing.

In meadows of green grass he lets me lie.
To the waters of repose he leads me;
  there he revives my soul.

He guides me by paths of virtue
  for the sake of his name.

Though I pass through a gloomy valley,
  I fear no harm;
beside me your rod and your staff
  are there, to hearten me.

You prepare a table before me
  under the eyes of my enemies;
you annoint my head with oil,
  my cup brims over.

Ah, how goodness and kindness pursue me,
  every day of my life;

> *my home, the house of Yahweh,*
> *as long as I live!'*

(Psalm 23)

What kind of day has your postmodern soul had so far? The writer of the twenty-third psalm has looked over his day and the very act of doing this has increased his faith in God, his love of self and others, his hope for the future. A most fortunate man, then, who sums up his mood with this simple statement of faith: 'The Lord is my shepherd, I lack nothing.'

No wonder this psalm is a favourite with so many of us. What a comfort it must have been to Jesus, both in the desert and in his daily life after the retreat. Who would not find the psalmist's response to life enviable, his trust in God inspiring – especially since it is clear that his day has not been without suffering? There has been joy and there has been sorrow for him. Goodness and kindness pursue him, but cannot remove those gloomy valleys through which he and we invariably pass. Like us, he faces danger and must deal with difficulties that seem determined to destroy him.

Psalm 23 touches on the whole spectrum of human experience and leaves space for us to bring to a meditation of it the particulars of our individual experience. The psalmist wrote it to express his own faith in God's goodness. Jesus may well have used it as the basis for prayerful reflection, both as he walked the paths of his desert retreat and as he sought to walk the 'paths of virtue' in his daily life. We too may find it a useful introduction to the grace of discernment we seek.

The psalmist reviews his day, recalling each moment and seeking to find the presence of God in both the joys and sorrows, the good and the not-so-good. It is the grace and skill of discernment that allows him to do this. I think Jesus did the same in those quiet moments when he left the crowds behind him and walked into the hills to pray. No doubt both men notice things said or done that, with hindsight and honest reflection, now cause sorrow or confusion. Neither of them were cast down by this, perhaps because they had the good sense to ask that God take everything of the day passed and use it for good. Ignatius recommends such a prayer for daily use during the Ignatian retreat:

> Grant me the Grace, O Lord
> That all my intentions, actions and operations
> May be directed purely to the praise and service of
>   Your Divine Majesty.

(Fleming, 1978)

It is a prayer that invites us, at the start of each day, to recollect everything of the previous 24 hours: the things we have done and the things we have left undone, our words and thoughts, the things that have happened to us and their effect on us. Recollecting as much of this as possible, we ask that all of it be used for God's purposes in this new day.

Our intentions are the plans and resolutions we make, along with the motivation for these – for example, Jesus intended, on hearing word of John's death, to take his disciples somewhere quiet where they could all come to terms with this sad news. I may intend to leave work promptly at five o'clock because too often these days my work has commanded every waking hour of my day to the detriment of family relationships. The things we intend, though, don't always come to pass.

Our actions are the things we actually do in the course of a day, along with our reasons for doing them. Jesus actually became deeply moved to see that a crowd had followed him and were looking so lost that he immediately began to teach them. I may actually leave the office at five o'clock as planned, but bring home a case full of work to keep me busy all evening.

That just leaves our operations – the variety of moods, emotions and thoughts that course through us unbidden, and often unnoticed, as we make our plans, succeed and fail to keep our resolutions, act and interact with events and people, sometimes masking our motives or mistaking our reasons. If Jesus was human he must have known every mood that we know. He too would have benefited from a careful examination of them all.

If we take time to review a day we will probably find that some of the things we have been up to can help us make discoveries about our true identity in God's love. But some of our intentions, actions and operations work against this – while a few are downright mystifying to us. The reason for the differences we observe is simple enough. Some of our intentions, actions and operations are directed towards God as the prayer suggests they should be. Others are directed more towards one or other of those addictions we explored in Chapter 4.

When we direct ourselves and our day to God we find, like the psalmist, that our soul is revived. Though life is still as difficult and painful as it always was, deep down there is a sense of authenticity; of being on the path of virtue. When, in some way, by thought, word and action, we direct ourselves away from God we step into confusion and frustration. No matter how good life seems on the surface, our soul is becoming parched, and our faith, hope and love grows weak. Try to think of an example of each direction from your own life; a time when you were 'in the flow' with God, as the writer of Psalm 23 is, and a time when you were out of step and out of sorts, as the writer (possibly the same writer) describes in Psalm 32:

> All the time I kept silent, my bones were wasting away
> with groans, day in, day out;
> day and night your hand
> lay heavy on me;
> my heart grew parched as stubble
> in summer drought.
>
> (Psalm 32.3–4)

Then notice how the psalmist goes on:

> At last I admitted to you I had sinned;
> no longer concealing my guilt,
> I said, 'I will go to Yahweh
> and confess my fault'.
> And you, you have forgiven the wrong I did,
> have pardoned my sin.
>
> (Psalm 32.5)

God is good and labours with whatever material we give him each day to fashion us as whole and holy people. If my basic desire is to co-operate with God's dream for me, I will find that I cannot turn away from God for too long without becoming dissatisfied. If this dissatisfaction can be examined with some honesty, it often reveals confusion – I have lost my way and now recognize this – and turns to sorrow. And thankfully sorrow is a grace and a sign, not of God's distance or disapproval or the hopelessness of my situation, but of God's concerned presence. Indeed, sorrow is often the first step we take towards God and away from whatever garden path had attracted the attention of our wandering feet.

Whenever we feel the heaviness of sorrow concerning the things we have done or the things we have left undone, we can take heart. God understands better – and with more compassion than we do – our difficulties and temptations, but God will not let us lie down (or give up on ourselves) until we reach those meadows of green grass and waters of true repose; until we too can say with joy: 'I lack nothing.'

With this assurance in mind take some time now to look over your day. What intentions, actions and operations can you recall? Re-play the events of the day like a video and, as you do, notice not just what was going on around you and to you, but what was happening within yourself. It takes some practice, but gradually you will be able to notice and name not just transient feelings, but deeper moods of peace, joy, encouragement, sadness, resentment, fear, anxiety, weariness, hurt, and so on. Give thanks for every feeling and mood you observe because God is now at work in them all to help you place your feet firmly on those paths of virtue that will bring you home to your authentic self. What kind of things in your day cause you to feel grateful as the psalmist does? And what gives you cause for regret? How might God be labouring in both your gratitude and your regret to grant you the grace of discernment, and how might you co-operate with this labour?

For example, I might notice that I was angry with my children this morning as I packed them off to school. What was going on? They were pretty much as usual: noisy, messy and reluctant to show any enthusiasm for my nutritionally balanced packed lunches. So what was new? A nun once told me that anger is our response to a felt lack of love, knowledge or power to do good. Perhaps I did not feel love towards my children this morning and that lack frightened me into anger. Perhaps I was frustrated by my inability to influence their behaviour around the breakfast table: 'How many times have I told you not to fire cornflakes at your sister?' Or perhaps I just could not find the solution to some problem I had fretted over all night. Around me everyone was doing the usual morning things, but without realizing it I felt bereft of something important. This perceived lack robbed me of equanimity, and in my confusion I responded with anger. The more I can understand my own anger the better placed I will be to ask for God's help in whatever area of need that I identify. For example, when it comes to my children I usually need help not to be a complete control freak.

Spiritual directors are mostly concerned to help a person notice which path they are taking, not just in the big decisions and choices of life such as career, but in the many little choices we all make every day. If we can begin to recognize which spirit is moving or motivating our intentions, actions and operations, and if we try to co-operate with the good spirit while resisting the not-so-good, then the big decisions, when they come, will not be so difficult to make.

However, the kind of consolation experienced by the psalmist when he says 'My home, the house of Yahweh, as long as I live!'(Psalm 23) is not the result of balancing the good with the regrettable in a daily review and finding that on balance his day has been directed towards God. The psalmist lacks no good thing not because he is perfect, but because he knows who he is and why he is here. He has discovered his own paths of virtue and walks them, however falteringly. What else is there to want in life? He surely lacks nothing, and in the face of life's joys and sorrows he is able to say: 'my cup brims over' (Psalm 23.5).

Psalm 23 reassures Jesus that, with the discovery of who he is before God and why he is vital to God's dream of wholeness, his cup too will brim over. He also will lack no good thing even if he should empty himself completely. He will understand, as the psalmist clearly did, how to live daily moments of action and interaction to the full, discovering through them his own paths of virtue. Paths that may lead him away from some things that are familiar and dear to him, but paths that will lead also to that deep peace that comes with just being at home with oneself, able to say, 'I am in the Father and the Father is in me' (John 14.11).

Jesus became a discerning person, able to distinguish a path of virtue from a garden path, and willing to choose the former for his feet. It is always a choice to say with the psalmist, 'Yahweh is my shepherd, I lack nothing', to be a discerning person. Jesus made this choice again and again as he threw his lot in with God, who creates good from everything that life can throw at us. God hopes we will do the same.

References

Fleming, SJ, David L., *Draw Me Into Your Friendship: The Spiritual Exercises. A Literal Translation and a Contemporary Reading.* St Louis, Institute of Jesuit Sources, 1996.

7

Faith in the Community

*Six days later, Jesus took with him Peter and James and his
brother John and led them up a high mountain where they
could be alone. There in their presence he was transfigured: his
face shone like the sun and his clothes became as white as the
light. Suddenly Moses and Elijah appeared to them; they were
talking with him. Then Peter spoke to Jesus. 'Lord,' he said 'it
is wonderful for us to be here; if you wish, I will make three
tents here, one for you, one for Moses and one for Elijah.' He
was still speaking when suddenly a bright cloud covered them
with shadow, and from the cloud there came a voice which said,
'This is my Son, the Beloved; he enjoys my favour. Listen to
him.' When they heard this, the disciples fell on their faces, overcome with fear. But Jesus came up and touched them. 'Stand
up,' he said 'do not be afraid.' And when they raised their eyes
they saw no one but only Jesus.*

(Matthew 17.1–8)

Whenever I am leading a residential retreat I always issue a
warning as the participants pack up to return home: 'Look
out for garden rakes.' Those who have been on retreat with
me before smile wryly, while others look puzzled. Let me
explain the garden rake phenomenon. Going away for a few

days' retreat is an ideal opportunity to rest, refresh tired bodies, minds and souls, and gain some perspective on life. This time away from our ordinary routine is beneficial, especially to busy people constantly serving family and friends. The kind of person who comes on retreat with me usually has many careful preparations to make for the folk back home before he or she can absent themselves even for 48 hours. But there comes a time to return home.

Ideally we will pack, alongside our belongings, some of the helpful resolutions we have made; the awareness of what it means to look after ourselves; perhaps even an insight that has been gained into our true desires and the choices we must make to become our most authentic selves. Suitcase stuffed with faith, hope and love, we head home only to walk into a domestic or work-related situation that is calculated (it seems) to undo in 30 seconds the good of the whole retreat. It feels just like stepping on a garden rake that has lain in wait and now deals a sudden and painful blow to the face.

A child has come down with chickenpox or fallen out of a tree. The washing-machine has sprung a leak or the roof has fallen in. At work a colleague waylays you with bad news before you have time to remove your coat. No one intends to bring you down to earth with a bang, though it should be remembered that those who stayed at home are feeling tired and irritable (just as you did three days ago) and the sight of your beatific face might bring out the worst in them. After all, they have not been where you have been. We may be feeling like new people, eager to tackle life with zest and creativity, but our partner, offspring and colleagues will not necessarily share our enthusiasm.

Now when I point out this obvious fact a chorus of groans usually arises and there is a general reluctance to complete the packing process. But it is vital to rejoin the crowd, to

71

come down from the mountain, leave the desert. Faith is not faith unless it is lived in the ordinary communities of which we are a unique and irreplaceable part. And none of us would be able to discover what our soul is telling us about our identity if we lived constantly in a desert of peace and tranquillity, isolated from real difficulties and real choices. No man or woman is meant to be an island, and we all need company and human intimacy if we are to become fully human – and therefore made in the image God has of us.

Jesus knew this; knew that he could not plumb the depths of his identity alone. After his retreat in the desert he wasted no time in seeking out and choosing to spend time with the kind of people who might populate any of our communities. Some of them were dreamers, some of them activists, some wealthy, others had to work hard to make a living. Gradually there formed around him a mixed company of men and women: married, single, employed and employers.

It is tempting for us to assume as we read the Gospels that these folk were selected from a much larger list of candidates for the post of apostle: that Jesus saw potential in each as leaders of the Church he was about to establish. We may imagine he chose Simon for his determination, Andrew for his loyalty, Philip for his integrity, and John for his literary genius. Perhaps Matthew would be a good treasurer, while the women could make colourful banners to adorn church walls. Even Judas had a role to play, however tragic.

We think like this not only because we know how things turned out, but also because we have the power to re-write the story to make it fit with the way things are now. The Gospel writers also did some editing, of course, and that is why only men are named as disciples in the Gospels – the woman being either relegated to the background or painted as sinners. Now Jesus didn't know how things would turn out. He formed his community not from people who would prove useful to a cause, but from people with whom he felt comfortable.

Perhaps he knew Matthew from childhood and enjoyed the acerbic humour the man doubtless displayed in his dealings with angry men grudgingly paying their taxes to him. Surely he sensed fun in the group of noisy fishermen complaining about the poor catch and joking together with their boss while mending nets in the early morning sun. And perhaps he found himself attracted to the passion of Judas – a man who loved God very much, if perhaps somewhat jealously, like Shakespeare's Othello who loved Desdemona 'Not wisely but too well'. Such passion might easily have struck a chord in Jesus, though perhaps a discordant one.

I imagine Jesus engaging in long conversations with Judas at night when all the other companions slept. I think he talked about what God was really like and the importance of interpreting Scripture in the light of that reality. Trying to warn Judas of the danger facing every zealot, every fundamentalist in whatever faith, of wielding holy scriptures as a weapon of indiscriminate and ruthless power to attain ends that never could be God's.

The point is this. If Jesus had run a selection process for the post of disciple, he would have come up with an entirely different crew from this bag of all-sorts he drew around him. But these were the people he wanted in his company. They were the ones he chose to come home to after a hard day of teaching or after an hour spent alone in prayer. Any garden rakes he walked into were left lying around by these men and women. Any insights he gained into his personal identity and the direction his life should take would not only come from this community of companions, but would involve them too. He had faith in the community he formed; that God could

73

and would work with it to help each member discover what life meant for him or her.

Hence the story in Matthew's Gospel of Jesus and three of his companions returning down the mountain after a religious experience that had transfigured Jesus and profoundly affected the three men with him. You will notice that these three did not want to leave the hill – perhaps they knew only too well that at the bottom a garden rake was already in position.

As they were rejoining the crowd a man came up to him and went down on his knees before him. 'Lord,' he said 'take pity on my son: he is a lunatic and in a wretched state; he is always falling into the fire or into the water. I took him to your disciples and they were unable to cure him.' 'Faithless and perverse generation!' Jesus said in reply 'How much longer must I be with you? How much longer must I put up with you? Bring him here to me.' And when Jesus rebuked it the devil came out of the boy who was cured from that moment.

Then the disciples came privately to Jesus. 'Why were we unable to cast it out?' they asked. He answered, 'Because you have little faith. I tell you solemnly, if your faith were the size of a mustard seed you could say to this mountain, "Move from here to there", and it would move; nothing would be impossible for you.' (Matthew 17.14–21)

The disciples were unable to cure the boy. It hit Jesus like a blow, and in confusion he watches his mountain-top experience melt away, leaving him to work out his salvation in the reality of this often exasperating community. Losing his cool completely, Jesus rounds on them all: the unfortunate father come to plead for help; the disciples shrugging their shoulders and hoping he will rescue them from this embarrassing situation; the milling crowd – not sure what is going on, but content to stay a while longer now that the Master has appeared on the scene. Even those simply passing by are included in the 'faithless and perverse generation' with which Jesus now takes voluble issue.

'How much longer must I be with you? How much longer must I put up with you?' he asks in exactly the same tone I might use towards my children as I clean up after them for the millionth time in any one week. Then, because someone needs help and that matters more than his frustration, he calls the sick boy to him and, without fuss, deals quickly with the cause of his disease. When order is restored, both to the boy's mind and to the gathered company, his disciples are not afraid to approach Jesus with a question. Like my children, they seem to understand that not everything that comes out of the mouth of Jesus needs to be taken to heart. Besides, they want to know where they went wrong in their attempts at deliverance. 'Why couldn't we cure that boy?' they ask, confused by their vague notions of how God works and, no doubt, full of chagrin at their failure to make him/her work for them.

The answer Jesus gives reverberates down the centuries, and is one that we all need to take to heart: 'I tell you solemnly, if your faith were the size of a mustard seed you could say to this mountain, "Move from here to there", and it would move; nothing would be impossible for you' (Matthew 17.20–21).

This well-known interaction is a very good example of the context in which Jesus made discoveries about himself, the world and the Father. Out of the chaos and frustration of community life, Jesus suddenly sees that God needs only a very little faith in order to do the impossible. He himself was near to despair a moment ago, yet the little faith he had was enough to cure the boy before him. And as Jesus responds to the disciples' question his spirit is back on top of the mountain, hearing his Father's voice: 'This is my Son, the Beloved; he enjoys my favour. Listen to him' (Matthew 17.5).

If *we* listen to what Jesus says in the gospel we will notice that mostly he is responding to these men and women questioning, searching, moaning about this and that. I don't think his responses came automatically. Each was an opportunity for Jesus to think through some issue concerning his identity and what God had in mind for creation. Ordinary conversations, careless remarks, passionate discussions – each helped him to discover more about himself and the purpose of his life. And each was a place of choice and of discernment.

When the mother of James and John came to secure for them places of honour, Jesus had a choice. Here was an opportunity to begin to build into this company a hierarchy of status and influence. Alternatively, he could listen to the still, small voice within that warned him against losing his soul in pursuit of some worldly kingdom and invited him instead to create a new kind of society. By choosing the latter he took another step towards his personal identity, and away from the expectations others had of him.

When you read a story from one of the Gospels try to imagine what was going on in Jesus. What choices faced him, which of his temptations might steer him away from the best choice? And, in retrospect, how did the choice he made affirm his identity as the Son?

Spend some time imagining what conversations might have been recorded if Jesus chose his companions from among our congregations, communities or families. My 14-year-old would have wanted to discuss with him the possibility and quality of life after death. My daughter would have complained about the injustices inflicted on the youngest in a family, while my 17-year-old would bemoan the responsibilities thrust upon the eldest. Using ordinary concerns like these, try to discover what Jesus would have wanted to share with each person in your own family about his understanding of life, death and relationships.

If Christ is alive and present in our church communities, then he is still living with a disparate bunch of individuals, grouped together in denominations that search vaguely and irregularly for a unity we call 'ecumenism'. Imagine a group of these pilgrims heading for Jerusalem, having arrived at Tel-Aviv airport six days ago to enjoy luxurious accommodation while they 'see the sights' and 'follow in the steps of Jesus', courtesy of Pilgrim Tours Inc. Now their air-conditioned coach whizzes along the road to Jerusalem while the occupants argue among themselves. Try to picture Jesus at the wheel listening attentively to the matter under heated discussion: what, according to Scripture, constitutes worship that is in spirit and in truth? Jean – a member of her local Pentecostal church – stands up with hands raised to heaven to insist that authentic worship is worship in tongues. John tells her not to be daft, worship is the celebration of the Mass – nothing more needed. That makes Alan extol the virtues, even the necessity, of some honest-to-goodness Bible exposition. Ruth dreamily offers her mantra 'inclusive language', which makes Frank shudder in fundamental disagreement. Patsy tries to encourage open-mindedness (which makes Frank shudder some more), and Phil, husband of Patsy and target of much well-meaning evangelism, dryly comments to anyone listening that the problem with religion has always been the religious people.

What is Jesus to make of this community? Try to imagine what he might say to them that would prove unforgettable. Perhaps he would tell them that with only a mustard seed of faith their minds and hearts could move every mountain that presently stood between them and true worship. That, in spite of their deep prejudices and private peccadilloes, they could be drawn together in praise and service of a bigger God than any of them had yet encountered if only they would let go of fear and let God transfigure them. Or perhaps he would say nothing, simply stopping the bus in the middle of the road and calmly announcing his intention to only drive on towards their destination, be it Jerusalem or the gathered Church of ecumenism, once the bickering ceased.

It is important to know the mind and heart of Jesus if we are to love him enough to follow him anywhere. We have at least as many concerns and difficult issues as those first disciples and we need to try and discern how Jesus might address them. Not to shore up our own position, though sadly this is what the gospel is often used for, but rather to become increasingly aware of what in human affairs concerns him and what does not.

For what concerns Jesus is usually a surprise to us. Have a look through the four Gospels or try to recall and make a list of all the questions Jesus is concerned to ask his companions and those he meets on his travels. 'Why are you sad?' Christ asks his fellow travellers on the road to Emmaus. 'What is it you are looking for? What is it that makes you doubt?' 'Why do you persecute me,' he asked Saul of Tarsus. Saul was finding it a little hard to believe that a man who lay in a tomb for three days could be alive and active as his friends were loudly claiming in every village square. Who do you say I am? What is it you want me to do for you? Jesus has always asked these questions, not to accuse and not from idle curiosity. These are questions of discernment – questions that might be asked by any spiritual director concerned to help a person listen to their own soul. Jesus asked such questions to help people discover for themselves who they are and what particular path or vocation in life would bring them peace. This was always his concern.

When Jesus told the story of the traveller who fell into the hands of robbers on the road to Jericho and of the three men who saw him lying injured, the question he asked was, 'Which of these three, do you think, proved himself a neighbour to the man who fell into the brigands' hands?' (Luke 10.36). The story came about because a lawyer had asked Jesus what he must do to inherit eternal life. Being advised by Jesus to love God with all his heart, soul, mind and strength, and his neighbour as himself, in accordance with the greatest commandment, the lawyer sought to justify his cavalier lifestyle by asking a supplementary question, 'And who is my neighbour?' (Luke 10.29).

Then Jesus told the story of the Good Samaritan and it became clear that he was not concerned to identify who had a claim on him, as the lawyer was. Jesus was interested in exploring for his own benefit and that of others what it meant to be a neighbour; what intentions, actions and operations were involved. The story he told makes it clear that for Jesus a 'neighbour' is a person with enough energy, compassion and will to turn aside from his or her plans and prejudices in order to help someone in need. When the lawyer saw this for himself, Jesus advises him to 'Go, and do the same yourself' (Luke 10.37). Seek to be a neighbour in all that you intend, in all of your actions, and in every thought, feeling, mood you allow to run unchecked through your heart, he tells the man. Sound advice.

Jesus was learning that when we offer help wherever it is needed, the neighbour we are assisting in turn assists us; becomes our Good Samaritan. He or she helps us in our quest to discover who we really are and what unique service we have to offer the world. Along with all the other people

Jesus met and those he lived with, this lawyer was helping him to become his true self (and in the case of some people, this was *in spite of* themselves).

The people we live and work and worship with can help us to do the same. Living in community nurtures neighbourliness. Neighbourliness is about reciprocity, and reciprocity is built into creation because for God wholeness is synonymous with holiness; when he works on one, she works on the other. It is this same reciprocity that makes it difficult to enjoy and discover God in the many good and related gifts of life while I am possessed or obsessed by any one of them. If only I had a mustard seed of faith to believe this.

With a mustard seed of faith I might see that it is the task of each member of a community to help other members recognize their personal identity. I cannot of course tell you who you are, only what I see you do. The disciples could see that Jesus had a gift of telling stories that explained to others what the kingdom of God was like, and a healing compassion that demonstrated what his stories described. Now our gifts are not our identity, but they are useful and readily available clues to it; they flow out from our truest, deepest self. All good gifts of personality, skill, talent, etc. come from God, so we can be sure that the particular gift or gifts we see in Jesus can tell us something about who he is for us. And we shall see in a later chapter that who he is for us is connected to who we are in and for him. When I look at Jesus I see him setting people free from so many things that keep them from enjoying life in all its fullness. What do you see him do?

It takes some practice to see and encourage each other's gifts. Again, your own family is a useful place to begin. Each member, young and old, has gifts. When we recognize a gift, value it, and encourage its expression, then we give the gifted person permission to claim and enjoy it as part of their true self. Can you recognize the gifts of each member of your family? In what ways are these being valued and allowed expression for the good of all?

Consider the social and political community of which you are a member. In what ways do the policies of the developed world at a local, national and international level sometimes help (but too often hinder) people to discover and express their gifts? Only a mustard seed of faith in the goodness of God is needed to help us see the gifts in the souls of our family, friends and neighbours; gifts that can transfigure this world of ours. Sadly we lack faith, so we do not see what the world could be.

Even in church communities we can become more concerned with tasks completed for the sake of the kingdom than of people liberated to be their true selves in that kingdom – almost as though God needed all our work and worry to complete creation. On the contrary, I am free to co-operate with God in the creation of the kingdom, but he/she can complete it without me and without my gifts of energy and enthusiasm, and certainly does not require my martyred service and guilt-driven duty.

My husband Jack once told his congregation the story of a grandfather working in his garden, planting daffodil bulbs. The man's three-year-old grandson arrives, donned in purple wellington boots and brandishing a plastic trowel with exultation. 'Can I help you, Papa? Let me plant some bulbs.' The grandfather straightens his sore back and looks at the child's shining face. He knows the job will take four times as long with this helper, and that there will be a lot of mess to clear up afterwards. But the child is keen, and the wise grandfather knows that both of them will derive a great deal of pleasure from this shared task of transfiguring the garden. The sun is warm, and there is really no hurry, so the two begin to work together. Eventually the bulbs are planted the right way up, the path is cleared, and the tools cleaned and stored safely. Two tired but happy figures survey the afternoon's labour with great satisfaction. 'That was fun. Can we do it again tomorrow?' asks the old man.

God does not need my assistance with creation, but has chosen to have it knowing that co-operating with God is very good for my soul. And, besides, God cannot help but enjoy my presence in this life!

Meanwhile, as I work and play alongside God and other searching souls in my communities of family, work and faith, the discovery of who I am and what gifts of service I can therefore offer the world will be ongoing. I am called to have faith in the community and in God who can make everything work to the good for those who love him, even garden rakes. Because Jesus had faith, he chose to live in community and God honoured this choice by revealing through ordinary men and women the will of God for him. But who could blame Jesus if just sometimes he thought longingly of the quiet of the desert and the inspiration of the mountain-top? Living with others has never been easy.

8

Travel Broadens the Mind

*He continued according to plan, traveled to town after town,
village after village, preaching God's kingdom, spreading the
Message. The Twelve were with him. There were also some
women in their company who had been healed of various evil
afflictions and illnesses: Mary, the one called Magdalene, from
whom seven demons had gone out; Joanna, wife of Chuza,
Herod's manager; and Susanna – along with many others who
used their considerable means to provide for the company.*

(Luke 8.1, Peterson, 1993)

Travel broadens the mind, or so they say. Long ago explorers
set out on perilous journeys to discover new lands; nowadays
we can have travel packaged for us to minimize the inconvenience and uncertainty of engaging with another culture
while maximizing the chance of sunshine or adventure.
We can also travel across the world without leaving our own
sitting-room. We can surf the net, or allow some television
personality to be our intrepid explorer by proxy. Books will
inform us about other cultures, other economic and political
systems, other religions. All this can broaden our minds too as
part of what we call education or lifelong learning. Evelyn
Underhill, at the age of 17, wrote: 'I hope my mind will not

grow tall to look down on things, but wide to embrace all sorts of things in the coming years' (Underhill, 1996 – an aspiration we all might adopt, and one that I think Jesus had too.

Jesus travelled. He made a journey from Nazareth to Jerusalem. We have no idea how many times in his 33 years he made the journey, but we know he did it at least twice, crossing from the region of Galilee into Samaria and back again. He also travelled around many of the towns and villages of Israel telling stories about God's kingdom, healing the sick, and provoking criticism from the religious leaders. What is not so obvious is the effect these travels and this engaging with people in streets and homes had on him. In what ways might the mind of Jesus have been broadened by what he saw as he travelled, not as a tourist imbibing briefly some scene before moving on to another amusement, but as one seeking to engage with people?

He met Jews of different schools and of varying passion, of course, along with Samaritans, Romans, Greeks, slaves, freemen, soldiers, women (that was new!), children, taxmen, lawyers, lepers, the whole strata of social class, rich, poor, sane, insane – a cosmos in miniature. He did not become disillusioned or cynical. His eyes were opened, and I am sure they were often hurt by much of what they saw, yet he did not despair. On the contrary, his experience served to strengthen his hunch that life had meaning and human life an inherent dignity.

We are left to piece together the mind of Jesus from the short snatches of his speech recorded in the Gospels, e.g. 'suffer the little children to come unto me and forbid them not'. If we give these statements only a cursory reading we may never know him at all. But if we expand those cryptic stories of Jesus meeting men, women and children on his travels, then we can catch a glimpse of the developing mind behind them. Here is a description by Paul Theroux of a happy encounter on the Grand Trunk Express:

Tamils are black and bony; they have thick straight hair and their teeth are prominent and glister from repeated scrubbings with peeled green twigs. Watch a Tamil going over his teeth with an eight-inch twig and you begin to wonder if he isn't trying to yank a branch out of his stomach. One of the attractions of the Grand Trunk Express is that its route takes in the forests of Madhya Pradesh, where the best toothbrush twigs are found; they are sold in bundles, bound like cheroots, at the stations in the province. Tamils are also modest. Before they change their clothes each makes a toga of his bed-sheet, and, hopping up and down and working his elbows, he kicks his shoes and trousers off, all the while babbling in that rippling speech that resembles the sputtering of a man singing in the shower. Tamils seem to talk incessantly – only toothbrushing silences them. Pleasure for a Tamil is discussing a large matter (life, truth, beauty, 'walues') over a large meal (very wet vegetables studded with chillies and capsicums, and served with damp *puris* and two mounds of glutinous rice). The Tamils were happy on the Grand Trunk Express: their language was spoken; their food was served; their belongings were dumped helter-skelter, giving the train the customary clutter of a Tamil home. (Theroux, 1990)

This is a delightful encounter not only with the Tamil culture, but also with the warmth and compassionate humour Paul Theroux employs whenever he writes about the idiosyncrasies of people all over the globe.

What might Jesus have written about his visit to a Samaritan village, assuming that, after meeting the Samaritan woman at the well, he was offered and accepted the hospitality of the villagers she brought out to meet him? Trying to imagine this will help you identify what you already know of the character of your Lord. It may also raise useful questions for further reflection. For example, perhaps Jesus would have written: 'Samaritans are the most extrovert of people. Their clothes are dyed in bold colours: blues and purples, reds and oranges. Their speech bulges with colourful adjectives. Their body language enthuses with dramatic gestures. The wide welcoming smile of a Samaritan is only a precursor to a huge embrace and loud acclamation of all that is most excellent about the day and this happy encounter.'

I have no idea of course what the Samaritan people were like. We know that they worshipped the same God as the Jews, shared the same scriptures, but had been rejected as impure by the Jews because of earlier intermarrying with foreign settlers. Not allowed a part to play in the rebuilding of the Temple by Ezra and Nehemiah, the Samaritans responded by building their own temple on Mount Gerizim, near the ancient city of Shechem. They were lost to the Jewish life for ever. The bitter enmity between Jews and Samaritans in the lifetime of Jesus was probably as irrational and unnecessary as the many religious conflicts in centuries following it. I think we can be fairly confident that it resulted in Samaria being to all intents and purposes a foreign land and culture to the young Jew from Nazareth. His exposure to these people would have been as fresh to the senses as was Paul Theroux's encounter with the Tamil gentlemen.

From the story of the Good Samaritan I get the impression that the Jews despised the Samaritans, tarred them all with the same brush: dishonest, unhygienic, and to be avoided at all costs. So I have had some fun redressing the balance here by imagining that Jesus found them to be colourful, extrovert, full of the joy of living, and generous with hospitality. The significance of the exercise does not lie in the accuracy of my portrait of the Samaritan villagers; rather, it highlights an awareness I have that Jesus did not 'move around the gospel' delivering stories and messages about God as a postman delivers mail. He was engaged by each person he met in a way that changed him. The question it raises for me is this: how is the risen Christ being changed through his encounters with the people living today? I think he was as delighted with this encounter at the Samarian well as Paul Theroux clearly was at his happy encounter with a group of Tamils on a train. Meeting the Samaritan woman broadened Jesus' Jewish mind.

Similarly, meeting the Greek woman from Syrian Phoenicia (Mark 7.24–30) broadened his vision. She wanted him to heal her daughter, and though he remonstrated at first because she was not a Jew and he was still making the traditional distinctions between Jews and Gentiles – understanding his mission to be one directed solely at his own people – she was insistent. Engaging him in a debate, she argued her case persuasively and with irresistible intelligence. In this good-humoured exchange Jesus found himself pushed by this clever woman beyond the boundaries he had thought existed for him. With a smile he acknowledged that perhaps he was not in the world only for the sake of the Jews, far less just male Jews, but for *all* men and women.

The Phoenician mother, concerned for a sick daughter, had sought an encounter with Jesus and that encounter had not only changed her life, but his. As any spiritual director might, she had called him to look beyond the parochial view of life he had inherited from Mary and Joseph to see the larger picture; a cosmic or world-view. If in her argument she had given him a passage of Scripture to reflect upon, it might have been Isaiah 54.2–3: 'Widen the space of your tent, stretch out your hangings freely, lengthen your ropes, make your pegs firm; for you will burst out to right and to left.' Here is an exuberant description of the hospitality God means all people to enjoy in the kingdom and an invitation to expand the boundaries of our welcome beyond traditional distinctions of race, creed, sexuality and gender; towards something universal and universally needed.

Jesus encountered different cultures as he travelled with his companions, and these encounters helped him to broaden the understanding and vision he had of his identity and God's purpose for his life. He also encountered the best and worst that humanity has to offer – rather like the investigative journalist John Pilger, who has spent his life exposing (in devastatingly understated prose) injustice, cruelty and cynicism. Here is one report written by Pilger in what, for me, is the spirit of Christ:

The football in Sonia's hands bears the picture and signature of Eric Cantona, together with the legend 'Eric the King'. Sonia is stitching the ball, which is her job in a village in India's Punjab. She is eleven years old and blind. She remembers the moment she lost her sight. 'It went completely dark in front of my eyes and I was scared,' she said.

She has since learned to stitch footballs by touch alone; her Aunt Satya matches up the panels and passes them to her niece. The two of them support an extended family since Sonia's mother fell seriously ill. When asked about the fun of being a child, Sonia said there was no fun in what she did. 'I have no choice'.

Before he retired from Manchester United in 1997, Eric Cantona earned around £19,000 a week, not including fees from advertising and commercial sponsorships, such as the use of his face and signature on footballs. In 1995–6, Britain imported £8 million's worth of sporting goods from India, made with cheap labour. Other European countries and the United States, Australia and Japan also 'out-sourced', as they say in the global economy, much of their sports manufacturing to untold numbers of Sonias in the poorest countries . . .

Globalization is a jargon term which journalists and politicians have made fashionable and which is often used in a positive sense to denote a 'global village' of 'free trade', hi-tech marvels and all kinds of possibilities that transcend class, historical experience and ideology. According to one of its chief proponents, Prime Minister Tony Blair, the very notion means that 'the grand ideological battles of the twentieth century are over'. What matters now, he says, are 'recovery' and 'growth', 'competitiveness' and 'flexible working'; all else is obsolete.

These terms could easily replace their equivalents in George Orwell's *1984*, for their true meaning is the dictionary opposite. Devoid of social and moral content, rather like the rows of Barbie dolls on the shelves of Hamley's toy supermarket in London, they point to the nightmare of ordinary people like Sonia and the toy workers, and to a class war waged at a distance by technocrats of the new Cold War. (Pilger, 1998)

Big business exploiting the poor, isn't that what the gospel tells us confronted the eyes of Jesus when he visited the Temple in Jerusalem? The teaching of Jesus is forgiveness of transgression, freedom from the state of guilt and from its influence. It seems on reading the Gospels that sins were not a big problem for Jesus. He forgave them in the Father's name, and it was a simple thing. 'Courage, my child! Your sins are forgiven' (Matthew 9.2), 'Your sins are forgiven . . . Your faith has saved you; go in peace' (Luke 7.48, 50). Temple business was based on a more elaborate system for salvation. It was a system that Jesus knew well and there is no reason to believe that he objected to it on the basis of its legality. Like the global economy and the free trade that oppresses Sonia in India, the Jewish Temple system of sacrifices was legal and even efficient. So what might Jesus write about after his famous visit to the Temple, when he is reported in the Gospels to have overturned the tables of the moneychangers? Imagine Jesus as a John Pilger. Compose for him a report of what met his eyes that morning in Jerusalem. Here is my attempt:

Outside children and old men beg for pity to be shown; a penny thrown at their outstretched hands. Inside big business has begun its daily sale of salvation. The whole Temple system of animal sacrifices perpetuates itself by proclaiming the constant necessity of ordinary people to atone for the latest breaking of the covenant which binds them to God and makes them righteous. To purchase atonement one buys an unblemished animal and lays upon it the task of mending the broken relationship. The innocent animal takes the consequences of the sin upon itself, and its blood is shed to atone for this sin. It becomes the scapegoat.

Since a person's relationship with God could be broken through disobedience, ignorance or even accident, no one is saved for long. These elaborate ceremonies and purges have no end; blood flows incessantly, day after day, in the Temple while the outer courts are noisy with the sound of bartering and exchange of various currencies for Temple coins.

Everywhere profits are being made, and legally made, in exchange for services provided to the many pilgrims who journey to Jerusalem. Those outside the Temple and the system, those with no money to purchase a propitiary offering, those sitting day after day begging for a merciful coin to be tossed in their direction, are the only losers. The Temple economy, like the salvation it offers, will never touch them. No wonder the religious leaders find it hard to accept that freedom from guilt could be not only accessible but final. No wonder they are hard pressed to decide which shocks them more when I heal a paralysed man or when I forgive him his sins. They know which will damage profits the more. I wonder what might happen to a man from Nazareth who suggests that the Temple system of sacrifices is about to become obsolete, those trafficking in scapegoats made redundant?

If I travelled with Paul Theroux or John Pilger I would not only learn a lot about these men, what they thought, how things affected them, etc., I would also learn to see the world through their eyes. By travelling around the gospel with Jesus we begin to know him more too. We learn that Jesus was a Jew who learned to widen the space of his tent. He also seemed determined to demonstrate that the sacrificial system, though it had served a purpose for centuries by allowing communication between man and God and God and man, was now redundant.

Both of these views remain relevant and radical today. There are striking similarities between the effect of big business on the lives of two-thirds of the world's citizens and the effect of the Temple system on those whose poverty and disease kept them outside that cult. With the destruction of the Temple and the dispersion of the Jews, the Jewish religion changed irrevocably of course. Isn't it strange, therefore, that we seem to have created another cult called 'globalization'?

In this new cult scapegoating is still very much in evidence. Consider the ethnic cleansing so recently and horrifically illustrated in Kosovo where an entire culture is made to bear the blame for historical sin, real or imagined, or for present economic difficulties. The Jewish people have themselves suffered throughout history as a convenient group upon whom could be heaped the blame for any disaster or difficulty occurring in the many countries they have adopted as home.

But of course there are subtler forms of sacrifice and scapegoating, of projecting our unease on to someone or some group outside our circle of society. Those who are different from us can quickly and conveniently become 'them': the new Samaritans. There are issues of unease and scapegoating closer to home even than Kosovo. In his book *Sex, Death and Punishment*, Richard Davenport-Hines quotes from the *Daily Express*, 13 December 1986, on the subject of AIDS:

> Yesterday an 89-year-old grandmother from Solihull rang us . . . 'The homosexuals who have brought this plague upon us should be locked up. Burning is too good for them. Bury them in a pit and pour on quick-lime' . . . the majority of Britons would appear to be in agreement. (Davenport-Hines, 1990)

It is tempting to blame some other when things go wrong or we are afraid. If we are really frightened or life becomes intolerable, we may even become as vicious as this grandmother. The same book quotes from Oscar Wilde, himself prosecuted in 1895 and publicly ruined because of the great sexual unease of British society – an unease that found a scapegoat in the homosexual. Wilde said:

> I have never come across anyone in whom the moral sense was dominant who was not heartless, cruel, vindictive, log-stupid and entirely lacking in the smallest sense of humanity. Moral people, as they are termed, are simple beasts. (Davenport-Hines, 1990)

Within every cult there is a moral code. If you step beyond the limits of the moral code I adhere to, I will become afraid. Fear can motivate me to become heartless, cruel, vindictive and log-stupid towards you. I may even experience a lack of the smallest sense of humanity; be more beast than human.

Strangely, I may act towards myself with the same outrageous cruelty whenever I feel afraid or separate from what my moral code tells me I should be. Then *I* become the scapegoat. I will sacrifice bits of myself to atone for my perceived sin. Sometimes I will even sacrifice my deepest most authentic self: my identity; my soul.

Hanging out with Jesus as he travels around not only the villages of Galilee, but the corners of my own life and experience, convinces me that this unasked-for sacrificing of self and others is redundant. God has no moral limit and therefore no moral outrage that needs to be placated. It is not possible for God to experience fear at any of the awful acts we are capable of perpetrating against ourselves, our neighbours and creation. Our God is a suffering God, his servant Jesus a suffering servant. God suffers our sin; when I move against my true self and the divine image in me, I move against God.

> For I am well aware of my faults,
> I have my sin constantly in mind,
> having sinned against none other than you,
> having done what you regard as wrong.
>
> (Psalm 51.3–4)

But Jesus taught that God neither retaliates nor demands reparation:

> Sacrifice gives you no pleasure,
> were I to offer holocaust, you would not have it.
> My sacrifice is this broken spirit,
> you will not scorn this crushed and broken heart.
>
> (Psalm 51.16–17)

God absorbs all our sins, rather like a large sponge absorbs spilled liquid until none is left and the surface is spotless.

> Have mercy on me, O God, in your goodness,
> in your great tenderness wipe away my faults;
> wash me clean of my guilt . . .
>
> (Psalm 51.1–2)

When Jesus visited the Temple he cleared it out not because there was some dishonest business practice going on, but because he had come to realize that the business itself was unnecessary. His travels had taught Jesus that God was too busy sponging up the sins of the world with an infinite capacity for compassionate understanding to be offended by them. Consequently, there was no point to all this trading in guilt. Humanity always was at one with its redeeming God, much as the prodigal son remained at one with the loving father even when the boy was farthest away from home. Because of God's unceasing labour, brought to completion in

94

the sacrifice of the beloved son, we always will be. To understand all is to forgive all.

Understanding all was the fruit of Jesus' travels and this is what led him to say on the cross, 'Father, forgive them; they don't know what they're doing' (Luke 23.34, Peterson, 1993). Passages of the gospel like this should carry a government health warning: beware – travelling with Jesus will broaden your mind too. For we are bound to be changed when we begin to connect the teaching and example of Jesus with the challenges we face in life, both as individual souls and as part of humanity at this precise moment in history. When we bring our arguments and concerns about life, liberty and the pursuit of happiness to a dialogue with Jesus, he will invite us to widen the hospitable space in us, just as his own space widened after meeting the Phoenician woman. He hopes we can extend the welcome we give both to our fellow travellers and to our own true self. For this will lead us to forgive ourselves and others as God has been forgiving us all along. We and Christ become like-minded in a process that never ends, for Christ continues to travel and to grow.

Vincent J. Donovan suggests that: 'Jesus of Nazareth grew into the Christ, or was made the Christ by God, at his resurrection. And since then the Christ has continued to grow – and grow' (Donovan, 1989). When Joan of Arc became a soldier, and when 200 years before that Francis of Assisi gave up soldiering to become the most gentle and nurturing of saints, Christ grew. When slavery was abolished and children were accorded human rights, Christ grew. When the Anglican Communion accepted that women could be priests, Christ grew. And when they accept women as bishops, Christ will grow again. With each growth comes a wider vision, a deeper understanding, not of imponderables like when Jesus of Nazareth became the Christ, but of who the Christ *now* is and what his concerns *now* are. For Donovan, it is an understanding that he believes is urgently needed. Looking at the whole of history from the birth of Jesus, he observes that:

> . . . after nearly two thousand years of Christianity, the Christ that is worshipped in our churches, the Christ that is the basis for our church and all its faith and life and activity, is no more than a Mediterranean Christ. That is as far as Christ has grown. European and American theologians see nothing wrong with that, nothing wrong with the fact that we have not even begun to think of, or search for, the meaning of a planetary Christ, a world Christ. We continue to let all our efforts revolve around a Mediterranean Christ. We of the West have monopolized Christ. (Donovan, 1989)

Christ must be allowed to keep travelling and growing into his identity. We cannot ask him to remain for ever the Christ that Luther knew; the one who brought reconciliation with God through freely dying on the cross to cover our guilt when we were helpless. He must be allowed to become the Christ of Liberation Theology, who empowers his followers to free themselves from oppression of every kind:

> The aim of the liberation process is to make our relationships with our neighbour be truly those of family and truly in solidarity, in order to enable us to live with dignity as children of God on all levels of human life (for we are biological, psychological, sociological, and spiritual). Thus we will be better able to relate to our Father and, in dealings with the other things of this earth, will be better able to learn to share with one another the goods of creation, with equity and justice.

By doing all this, we will make our planet a true home where we can live in a human fashion and a genuine passageway to eternity. (Jaen, 1991)

There is growth even beyond this, of course, and Christ still needs the help of companions if he is to become the Christ for the third millennium, the cosmic Christ. For, as Sister Teresa of Avila wrote:

Christ has no body now on earth but yours,
no hands but yours, no feet but yours;
Yours are the eyes through which is to look at Christ's
compassion on the world,
Yours are the feet with which he is
to go about doing good
and yours are the hands with which
he is to bless us now.

I suspect that the hands with which Christ chooses to bless us now are those of men and women in every country and of every religion and situation. Christ grows into his own true identity whenever any of us travel through life, being attentive to our soul as we engage with each situation, every encounter, with integrity. How prepared are you to be part of this company of all-sorts? What grace will you need to travel with these others, and how might you accept their help in the discovery of your unique self and the demands of love upon you? I suggest we will all need the grace of a deep awareness that God can be found in everything and that 'there are no more distinctions between Jew and Greek, slave and free, male and female, but all of you are one in Christ Jesus' (Galatians 3.28).

References

Davenport-Hines, Richard, *Sex, Death and Punishment*. London, Collins, 1990.

Donovan, Vincent J., *The Church in the Midst of Creation*. London, SCM Press, 1989.

Fleming, SJ, David L., *Draw Me Into Your Friendship: The Spiritual Exercises. A Literal Translation and a Contemporary Reading*. St Louis, Institute of Jesuit Sources, 1996.

Jaen, SJ, Nesto, *Toward a Liberation Spirituality*. Chicago, Loyola University Press, 1991.

Petersen, Eugene, *The Message*. Colorado, NavPress Publishing Group, 1993.

Pilger, John, *Hidden Agendas*. London, Vintage, 1998.

Theroux, Paul, *Travelling the World*. London, Sinclair-Stevenson, 1990.

Underhill, Evelyn, *The Spiritual Life*. London, Hodder & Stoughton, 1996.

9

Soul Brother, Soul Sister

> *... and there are no more distinctions between Jew and Greek,*
> *slave and free, male and female, but all of you are one in Christ*
> *Jesus. Merely by belonging to Christ you are the posterity of*
> *Abraham, the heirs he was promised.*
>
> (Galatians 3.28–9)

These words were written by Paul in a letter to the church at
Galatia in AD 52. What Paul knew he had learned from Jesus,
who appeared to him as the risen Christ. Both men lived and
died during a time when many distinctions were made
between one human being and another according to race,
religion, class and gender. By the time he wrote his letter to
Galatia, Paul had come to understand such distinctions to be
man-made. He could see that God, being infinite, has all the
time in the world – and all the possibilities too – and therefore no need to select one created thing over another. Paul
had not always thought this way, though. Saul of Tarsus, as he
had been previously known, had been a man of faith and
fervour who listened unconvinced as Stephen claimed before
the High Council that Jesus from Nazareth had been raised
from the dead by God. Saul did not waver in this disbelief as
he held the coats of those determined to stone Stephen to

death for blasphemy, even congratulating them on their murderous actions. Soon after this, Saul was on the road to Damascus, blinkered by his own religious convictions and zealously pursuing the followers of Jesus in order to arrest them for trial in Jerusalem.

Conversion came when he encountered Jesus on that road. Imagine his surprise that this dead carpenter had the audacity not only to be alive, but to address a rather pointed question: 'Saul, Saul, why are you out to get me?' (Acts 9.4, Peterson, 1993) Christ asked. Perhaps Saul was busy persecuting so many people that he could not be sure which one of them now accused him, because he responded with a question of his own: 'Who are you Master?' (Acts 9.5, Peterson, 1993) Jesus replies: 'I am Jesus, the One you're hunting down. I want you to get up and enter the city. In the city you'll be told what to do next' (Acts 9.5–6, Peterson, 1993).

It was at that moment that Saul discovered that he was stone blind, physically as well as spiritually. He had to allow his companions to lead him into Damascus, the town to which he had so recently pursued his quarry, anticipating total victory over them. There Paul spent many hours in prayer and made two discoveries. First, he discovered that the risen Jesus he had encountered in that dramatic vision on the road could also be encountered, just as vitally, in quiet prayer. Second, Paul discovered that encountering Christ regularly, getting to know his mind, talking intimately as one friend to another about his own concerns and sorrows, could turn one's world upside down. Encountering the risen Christ in prayer is possible for us all. Through prayer, especially perhaps when we contemplate the gospel, we can learn from Christ what our infinite God is like. This, after all, is what Jesus was concerned to reveal.

As Paul surrendered himself to his own *kenosis*, he began

to see things through God's eyes. He glimpsed the truth that God has no limitations and no favourites. That the Creator sees the whole of creation as desirable and intends to have it all: Jew and Greek, slave and free, male and female: 'God saw all he had made, and indeed it was very good' (Genesis 1.31). Paul draws on this insight for his letter to the church of Galatia, describing a vision for humanity that was new and controversial. A vision that needed to be caught if Christ was to grow from being a Judeo-Christian saviour into the saviour of the Gentile world with which Paul was now engaged.

Naturally it took Paul some time to grow fully into that wider vision of what faith means, just as it took all of Jesus' life for him to become God's Word and meaning (*logos*). No doubt both began their adult lives saying the prayer that every male Jew offered daily: a prayer of thanksgiving that he was not born a Gentile, a slave or a woman. But if you prayerfully follow Jesus around the villages, meeting the men and women, Jews, Samaritans and Romans he met, I think you will see a man growing out of this and every other stereotypical response to life into a freedom enjoyed by God and meant for us all. We too need to grow more fully into the grace of being one in Jesus Christ, and Jesus can help us. If it were not so, I do not believe that Paul, had he lived for three lifetimes, could have come to see that God does not make, and never made, the kind of distinctions he addresses in his Galatian letter.

Recall the Roman centurion whose servant was ill. Jesus offers to visit the house, and would have done so as easily as he visited Peter's house to heal his mother-in-law, had the centurion's faith not made this unnecessary. Or take the meeting between Jesus and the rich young ruler; he, you will remember, approaches Jesus with all the assurance of his station in life:

He was setting out on a journey when a man ran up, knelt before him and put this question to him, 'Good master, what must I do to inherit eternal life?' Jesus said to him, 'Why do you call me good? No one is good but God alone. You know the commandments: You must not kill; You must not commit adultery; You must not steal; You must not bring false witness; You must not defraud; Honour your father and mother.' And he said to him, 'Master, I have kept all these from my earliest days.' Jesus looked steadily at him and loved him, and he said, 'There is one thing you lack. Go and sell everything you own and give the money to the poor, and you will have treasure in heaven; then come, follow me.' But his face fell at these words and he went away sad, for he was a man of great wealth. (Mark 10.17–22)

He knows himself to be a righteous person and so this young man is not afraid to run up to Jesus. Kneeling squarely in front of the Master, he articulately states his case, confident that he understands the requirements of God's laws. So he nods eagerly as Jesus lists some of them, for he not only knew what was right but he *did* what was right, and consequently God had blessed him with wealth. He has come to meet Jesus not to learn how to live, but to negotiate the question of eternal life. His wealth and station already guarantee him freedom beyond the wildest dreams of any slave. Still it seems he has a nagging concern that there is yet something missing. What else must I do, he wants to know, to be sure that I have secured for myself the right to eternal life?

This man is not the first or last to find himself preoccupied with a sense that there must be something more to the life of faith. People come for spiritual direction with this same hunch. They have lived the religious life for many years and yet they sense that something important still lies just beyond the periphery of their vision. Not everyone seeks an answer in the same place, of course. Some try to satisfy a longing for eternity by leaving their mark on *this* world. They want to be somehow like Abraham – the father of a nation that will live for ever. So they pursue success, either worldly or religious; wealth, or a wealth of piety, fame or a famous faith; power, or a seat of influence in the congregation; the right to be remembered for ever.

Whichever was true here, Jesus was drawn to the young man's candour and so tells him what he himself has learned to be true. All the wealth in the world, and all the righteousness possible before the Law, count for nothing if a person is enslaved to them. Then Jesus makes an offer: sell all your dreams of worldly immortality and success, he invites, and be generous with the money, time and energy this down-sizing will realize, and come; leave behind your ideas of what makes a man right with God. Come and learn from me what it means to be truly free and truly alive in the here and now.

His answer shatters the youth, leaving him speechless as only *kenosis* can. The rich young ruler turns away sadly because his possessions, including his ideas of himself and his image of a God who rewards his favourites with wealth and position, were great and were in complete possession of him. Jesus was sad too. He could see that the young man feared he was being offered little in exchange for his great financial and religious wealth; slavery in exchange for freedom. The real wealth of the man, the freedom to be his own true self in the service of God, lay undiscovered like the pearl it was.

Down through the ages individuals have tried to negotiate this business of eternity with God, confident as the rich young man in a belief that God must want to negotiate with them.

Nothing could be further from the truth. God is not interested in eternity-for-a-few, but in wholeness-in-Christ for all. Still we insist on being selective and making distinctions, especially between men who would negotiate, and women historically excluded from all negotiations, by a form of discrimination so ancient that it is intrinsic to both class and religion.

> Now there was a woman who had suffered from a haemorrhage for twelve years; after long and painful treatment under various doctors, she had spent all she had without being any better for it, in fact, she was getting worse. She had heard about Jesus, and she came up behind him through the crowd and touched his cloak. 'If I can touch even his clothes,' she had told herself 'I shall be well again.' (Mark 5.25–8)

In stark contrast to the wealthy man, this woman approaches Jesus in desperation: desperate to be well and desperate not to be seen. She knows she is breaking the Levitical Law by being in the street among people. While the wealthy man is confident in his righteousness before the Law, she feels condemned by it.

The earliest cultic injunction or taboo concerned the dangerous nature of blood and the need to contain its power. It was believed that the blood of a person contained that person's life-force. If a person bled they were expected to die, unless some dangerous magic was at work. Later Hebrew Law stated that the blood belonged specially to God, so when a man or woman shed human blood they severed the union between themselves and God. This too was dangerous. In the interests of public safety they must be removed from the religious community before their uncleanness could contaminate others. After a specified period of time a religious ceremony of atonement would take place to repair the break between God and man or woman, allowing the person to rejoin the cult and community.

The book of Leviticus gives specific instructions regarding the duration of a woman's ritual uncleanness both during – and for some time after – her menstrual flow, and also after childbirth. These instructions made no comment on the woman's moral, ethical or even her devotional condition. They were not intended to nurture in her a sense of being rejected by God. It was simply that the flow of blood regularly put the woman outside the cult, and atonement was required to bring her back in again. Naturally this to-ing and fro-ing meant that women were distinctly less able than men to take part in religious matters – one more reason for being considered second-class citizens of their society.

Centuries later, the woman in Matthew's Gospel feels pain and panic each time she brushes against another person in the street. Pain because of her own sinfulness before the Law, panic at the fear of discovery, and the shame and punishment that would bring. So she approaches hesitantly, from behind, screwing up her courage to reach out for that touch of his cloak that will surely make her well.

A few years ago I found myself leading a discussion entitled 'Once a Month' for a group of ten women interested in exploring a female spirituality. We began by reading what the Bible writers had said on the subject of blood, and soon found ourselves wondering if women still thought of themselves as outside their own faith community in some way. Looking at the Church it seemed possible that men and women are still inclined to exclude women from positions of leadership because they have not grown entirely free from an ancient and deep-seated fear of blood. How exactly, we wondered, did issues of blood still exert control on twentieth-century women and men, and what might Jesus be saying to them about it?

A simple relaxation exercise helped us to become attentive to those operations Ignatius speaks of (see Chapter 6), that are going on within us all the time. Then I invited the women to become aware of their own feelings and reactions as we read aloud these verses from Leviticus:

> When a woman has a discharge of blood, and blood flows from her body, this uncleanness of her monthly periods shall last for seven days. Anyone who touches her will be unclean until evening. Any bed she lies on in this state will be unclean; any seat she sits on will be unclean. Anyone who touches her bed must wash his clothing and wash himself and will be unclean until evening. Anyone who touches any seat she has sat on must wash his clothing and wash himself and will be unclean until evening. If there is anything on the bed or on the chair on which she sat, anyone who touches it will be unclean until evening. (Leviticus 15.19–23)

Without comment, we went on to listen to a moving song about the woman with the haemorrhage and the state she found herself in as she approached Jesus in the street. As the woman's story of fear and shame unfolded I placed an open Bible on the table, and on top an unused, still-wrapped, tampon. Quietly I posed the question: 'Where is the clean, and where is the unclean?'

I had been aware of anger and hurt sweeping round the group during the reading from Leviticus, and of a wave of compassion during the song. Now I saw shock, even fear, on the faces of these women as they saw what I had done. When it comes to blood we are all, it seems, still Old Testament women. Although personal hygiene advances have freed us all to live normal lives during menstruation, the unconscious compulsion to conceal and separate our menstrual cycle from our devotional life may remain, unseen, to exert its power. What hope, then, for a female expression of spirituality?

All of us looking on the tampon that October night clearly understood that there is no magic needed to explain why a women bleeds, but does not die. No current taboo is broken by a menstruating woman and no guilt or shame is attached to her. But before our audible gasps had subsided and we had reassured ourselves with these thoughts, the door to our meeting room opened and the parish priest, whose house we were using, popped his head around to ask if we were comfortable. Irony indeed. Or was the providence of God pressing home to us the point that we are all still as disabled by that ancient blood issue as the woman in the gospel? Even I, who was prepared at least for the sight of a tampon on top of a Bible, was anything but comfortable as I willed the priest not to glance at the table. This was taboo.

Later on, when our collective blood pressure had returned to something like normal, we shared in the group our experiences of that hidden rite of passage – the first period. There was both laughter and sadness at the absurdity of 'the curse', the irony of 'your friend', the shame and fear and darkness of so much of our nurture at a vulnerable age. One woman told how totally unprepared she was for that first period. She was 12 years old and thought she was bleeding to death. Another hid her soiled underwear in the laundry basket and prayed that whatever this illness was it would just go away again. Next day a packet of sanitary towels appeared on her bed, and thereafter every month a new packet of towels appeared. No word was spoken between parents and daughter.

There were more encouraging memories too amid the

strict instructions not to wash hair during a period and not to do any exercise. It was good to see sanitary towels now advertized on television, but wryly we observed that the selling point for them was often their invisibility. Was this a modern take on the old taboo? Were we being told that no woman needs to hide away from decent society when she is bleeding, so long as no one knows she is bleeding? Certainly no one could guess that the smiling woman in skintight trousers skipping elegantly around a tennis court has period cramp, a bloated stomach (how does she even fit into those trousers?) and a headache, feels a bit weepy and uncoordinated, and on top of all this is bleeding. The product must be very good indeed to mop up all of these – as well it should be, given that in Europe at least the sanitary towel is considered to be an item of luxury and women obliged to pay tax on each purchase. To tax a woman for menstruating – isn't that disturbingly akin to the sacrificial offering required in the Hebrew ceremony of atonement?

So our musings continued, and since this was a discussion in the context of spirituality we finally turned to the question Jesus might ask: 'What is it that you want?' We wanted to celebrate with our daughters and grand-daughters the important event of the first period. A shopping expedition, a special lunch in a fashionable restaurant, a simple liturgy in the home, were all suggestions put forward. We wanted to acknowledge that women have struggled for centuries to approach Jesus through a hostile crowd of religious and secular laws, crippled by an ancient unease that has proved incurable. Indeed, that women like us (and most women in this group were Catholic) can still come to prayer with the feeling clinging to us that we are outside, or at least on the periphery, of God's kingdom, sidelined from what God has in mind for creation and humanity. Laws blatantly restricting our choices and oppressing our rights may have been removed, but too often they are replaced with glass ceilings, even in the Church. We wanted to break through taboo, celebrate the faith of women in new ways, declare her to be clean – even sacred. Above all, we wanted Christ to empower us for the liberation process still unfinished, as Jesus did the woman he met at the well (John 4.7–29).

Distinctions had been drawn that had trapped this woman in a poverty of aspiration. She seemed content, or at least resigned, to be passed from one man to another in order presumably to earn a crust by fulfilling the only role (as man's comforter) open to her in the society of her day. Her soul was the soul of an evangelist, but this truth lay hidden under years of neglect, mistaken choices, and the denial of her most basic right to be fully human and self-determining. Women who reflect prayerfully on this encounter often discover that it's not what Jesus and the woman discuss that is significant to her or to them. The pair talk of water and domestic arrangements and worship. It is the fact that he talks to her at all that blows the minds of many women who have faithfully attended our Christian churches for decades, only to be addressed there in the most surreal fashion as 'soldiers of Christ' or (in many subtle ways) as some doorway to evil.

In *The Heart of the Enlightened* Anthony de Mello (de Mello, 1989) tells the story of a family out to dinner in a restaurant. The waitress comes to take the order. The youngest boy asks if he may have a hot dog, but his mother, feeling that she knows best what is good for her son, tells the waitress to bring him steak and potatoes and vegetables. The waitress then turns to the boy and enquires, 'Would you like ketchup or mustard on your hot dog?' Ketchup is the boy's preference and, as the waitress turns away to attend to the order, he whispers to his stunned family: 'She thinks I'm real!'

109

Jesus thought the woman at the well was real – that she really mattered. Her fears and hopes, her dreams and sorrows, all mattered. He asks real and pertinent questions; not prying in order to accuse, but helping her to recognize and pay attention to the reality of the background unhappiness she feels about her predicament and problems. Suddenly, coping with it all – as she has done for so many years – will no longer suffice. Because Jesus makes no distinction between her and a person with a right to a life before death, she also is encouraged to stop making that distinction. No wonder she runs to tell her neighbours and friends to quit their work and to come and meet this man. Women often introduce their friends, both female and male, to spiritual direction in the same exuberant way as the Samaritan woman ushered her neighbours out to the well.

But what happened next? I have no way of knowing whether the woman left her village to accompany Jesus to Jerusalem, or simply followed news of him. I cannot say if the rich young man thought better of his choice and caught up with the company a little later. I do, however, know what happens to men and women as they encounter Jesus in prayer.

He speaks directly into the person's situation, calling them real, and calling them by name into a life of unique creativity and intimate fellowship with him. Come, follow me; leave behind your wealth of prejudices about life and your poverty of aspirations. Come and discover from me the truth about yourself and God, truth that will set your soul free.

Like the disciples before them, praying people are drawn to this invitation: they long to leave everything and follow him. But notice that even after three years of close companionship, the disciples' loyalty to Jesus is easily shaken and at any sign of danger they are ready to turn for home. For them, as for us, the good news about what God has in mind can seem just too good to be true and too radical to be always attractive. What finally makes the difference for friends like Peter and Mary, Nicodemus and Martha, and later for Paul on the road to Damascus, was not what Jesus taught or what he did. It was who he was. For his part, Jesus knew better than they that no man, however charismatic, could ever free them from all that held them captive to the status quo of race, class and gender. Only a saviour could do that.

Reference

de Mello, Anthony, *The Heart of the Enlightened*. London, Fount, 1989.

10

The Rock and the Stonemover

When Jesus came to the region of Caesarea Philippi he put this question to his disciples, 'Who do people say the Son of Man is?' And they said, 'Some say he is John the Baptist, some Elijah, and others Jeremiah or one of the prophets'. 'But you,' he said 'who do you say I am?' Then Simon Peter spoke up, 'You are the Christ,' he said 'the Son of the living God'.

(Matthew 16.13–16)

It was the same question we are all tempted to ask: 'Who do people say that I am?' Not simply because we are addicted to the approval that others can give or withhold, but because we all develop in childhood a tendency to become who the influential people in our lives say we can become. Even now that I am grown, if people say that I am a talented and lovable human being, then quite likely I will discover many talents within and develop into a loving and confident individual. However, telling me that I am a no-good nuisance will make it difficult for me to become anything other than a social misfit and a desperately unhappy person, especially if this is reinforcing a message I heard often as a child. As we have seen, our earliest experiences, including what people say about us, form a first principle within us, a foundation for all that follows. These experiences and how we have perceived them give us a powerful and often hidden image of who we are and what life means. An image that can shape our lives and limit our horizons.

And if what family, friends, teachers and colleagues say about us is influential, then how much more powerful is what society as a whole says about groups of us: women are second-class citizens and 'unclean'; gay people are perverts; anyone who is different is 'them', not 'us', and can be treated as strangers. Society has said all of these things at one time or another and, worse still, has acted (and even legislated) upon such pronouncements.

At this point in the story of Jesus, what people think of him is of considerable importance. Things are becoming dangerous, and if the crowd turn against him on a whim they could unwittingly destroy him. Besides, Jesus was a man much like any other: connected to and affected by the thoughts, feelings and opinions of those around him. He was a wise man too, who knew the danger of being the sole judge of one's life and work. He had travelled from village to village, met people, listened to their stories, encouraged them, and challenged and helped them to make sense of their experience in the light of Love. Now he wondered how it had all been received. Without the benefit of newspapers circulating in Palestine to make their comments on the Jesus phenomenon, he had to turn to his closest companions for help.

Around the Lake of Galilee, folk were certainly talking about Jesus: his background, his sudden appearance at the side of John, followed by his equally sudden disappearance. Everyone felt themselves connected to at least one Jesus story. I was the aunt of the boy with the loaves and fishes at that extraordinary picnic. My neighbour's wee lass was all but dead, when Jesus paid a visit and within minutes had her sitting up and eating soup. I was just passing on my way to Jerusalem with my caravan of spices when the commotion at Lazarus' house caused a traffic jam that held me back for two days.

So when Jesus asked his friends how he was viewed, they explained to him that popular opinion thought he was the prophet Elijah reappeared. Perhaps Jesus smiled at this before asking what he really needed to know: 'And how about you? Who do you say I am?', for Jesus was able to judge between the transitory notions of an optimistic or desperate populace and the intimate knowledge of close friends.

Important as it was for him to be forewarned about how his message and person were being perceived at large, and what expectations the crowd had of him, it was even more important for him to find out from this small company of men and women their *knowing* of him. He hoped that they, at least, might love him sufficiently to lay aside their own dreams of what he could be, and do, for them long enough to help him in this crucial matter of his personal identity.

As usual, it is Simon who speaks for them all. Hearing Jesus' question, he searches within himself for words that might capture what he felt to be true about this man from Nazareth. It is Simon's unfettered soul that knows the answer to the question 'Who is Jesus for me?' He speaks and, hearing his own words, recognizes the truth of them. What he says has become the most familiar verse of Scripture: 'You are the Christ . . . the Son of the Living God' (Matthew 16.17).

Watching Simon's face, listening to him speak this simple truth, affects Jesus profoundly. In one instant his life is shattered into a thousand bright pieces and re-membered into one luminous word: Christ. Herein lies the meaning, the purpose, and the goal of Jesus' life. Every moment has pointed to this, every breath has led to it. This is what pulled him away

114

from the carpenter's bench. This is what drew him to the waters of his baptism, and then on through the silent desert into towns and villages and the lives of everyone he met. And now this word would draw him to the city of Jerusalem and on to a cross at Calgary. He is Jesus the Christ, the Word of God uttered from the very beginning; God's *Logos* (meaning) for creation. His coming into the world, his willingness to live the fullness of humanity in freedom and service to God, would bring that meaning to its fulfilment, beginning of course with Simon.

From a heart filled with the gratitude of confirmation, Jesus tells the fisherman:

> God bless you, Simon, son of Jonah! You didn't get that answer out of books or from teachers. My Father in heaven, God himself, let you in on this secret of who I really am. And now I'm going to tell you who you are, *really* are. You are Peter, a rock. This is the rock on which I will put together my church, a church so expansive with energy that not even the gates of hell will be able to keep it out. (Matthew 16.17–18, Peterson, 1993)

Peter does not object to the vocation suddenly laid upon him. There is no need. At the precise moment when he recognized who Jesus was for him, Peter also knew who he himself was. In his soul he recognizes that he is indeed the Rock. Perhaps he remembers being in at the foundation of other projects throughout his life, and of being steady in times of crisis, solid in his friendships. Now Peter sees what Jesus sees – that he has indeed laid the foundation of a belief in Jesus as God's Word incarnate. With his confession, Peter has fulfilled the promise God saw in him from before his birth. And it felt like coming home to himself.

The Christ and the Rock – two men, very different in personality, temperament and vision – help one another to discover the most intimate truth about themselves, their own personal Word of life. A Word that made sense of experience and longings, an identity that brought into focus the purpose of life, a salvation to live by, and for which a person might even choose to die.

Herbert Alphonso SJ believes that Ignatius' Spiritual Exercises are intended to help a person discern their truest and deepest self: who Christ says they are. Vital to that discernment is the discovery Peter made of who Jesus is for us. Alphonso tells the story of a middle-aged Jesuit who came to speak to him about his prayer:

> He shared with me that he had not been praying for many years: even if he did go to prayer – very rarely, he said – he actually did not pray; he was present only bodily, materially. As he spoke of his great negligence in prayer, I got the feeling that he was sort of 'hung up' on his negligence in prayer. So I sensed that if I had to be of help to him, I had first to make him take his distance from this 'negligence in prayer' with which he was somewhat obsessed, to look at it in perspective. So I said to him: 'You haven't been praying for a long, long time. Tell me: have you at any time in your life felt spontaneously close to God – not because you went through a reasoned process, but spontaneously, have you ever felt your heart uplifted and yourself in touch with God, in union with God?' I had hardly framed the question when he said: 'Of course, whenever I look back at my past life and see how good God has been to me, I feel immediately close to God, in touch with God, united with Him.' (Alphonso, 1993)

Being an experienced spiritual director Alphonso noticed that the Jesuit had come alive; his negligence was forgotten and he was now talking with deep feeling and a sparkle in his eyes. So Alphonso reflected this back to him, observing that the goodness of God seemed to mean a great deal to the priest, and enquiring if he had ever taken that attribute as a focus for his own prayer. When the priest said he had never prayed on the goodness of God and even questioned just how long he could be expected to pray on one single theme without growing tired, Alphonso suggested that he try it and see.

Notice in the defensive reaction of this Jesuit, a spirit other than God's trying hard to stop him in his tracks. He has come seeking help for his prayer life, but now that help is at hand, the man wants to change his mind, back off, prevaricate. He hides this resistance by suggesting that to pray on the goodness of God is too simplistic to be effective. I am reminded of Naaman, the army commander who visited Elisha having heard that he could heal his leprosy. Naaman took with him gold, silver and fine robes to pay for his cure, but Elisha, not even bothering to come out and meet Naaman, sent word instead that he should go and bathe in the River Jordan to be cured of his leprosy:

> But Naaman was indignant and went off, saying, 'Here was I thinking he would be sure to come out to me, and stand there, and call on the name of Yahweh his God, and wave his hand over the spot and cure the leprous part. Surely Abana and Pharpar, the rivers of Damascus, are better than any water in Israel? Could I not bathe in them and become clean?' And he turned round and went off in a rage. But his servants approached him and said, 'My father, if the prophet had asked you to do something difficult, would you not have done it? All the

more reason, then, when he says to you, "Bathe, and you will become clean".' So he went and immersed himself seven times in the Jordan, as Elisha had told him to do. And his flesh became clean once more like the flesh of a little child. (2 Kings 5.11–14)

The priest who visited Alphonso thought his negligence in prayer was a form of leprosy. God must surely recoil in horror from him until, with great difficulty and no little cost, a cure could be found. What an affront to suggest that simply praying as he can – that is, contemplating the goodness of God – and leaving to others the kind of prayer he could not manage would make him whole and holy; would allow him to approach prayer (as Jesus suggests we all should) with the integrity of a little child.

Five months later the two men met again and, excited as any child, the middle-aged Jesuit told Alphonso what he had discovered in that time: 'Herbie, I can pray *always* on the goodness of God' (Alphonso, 1993). Contemplating the goodness of God, he had discovered, was not only the secret of his prayer, but of his life of service too, along with his relationships and even his relaxation and recreation. It was a holistic prayer because the personal identity is not what a person does, but rather what that person means to Christ. Here is how Alphonso explains this:

So all vocations are in Christ Jesus: the personality of Christ Jesus is so infinitely rich that it embraces all calls and vocations. If then each of us has a 'personal vocation', this can only be in Christ Jesus. This means that there is a facet of the personality of Christ Jesus, a 'face' of Christ Jesus, which is proper to each one of us, so that each one of us can in very truth speak of '*my* Jesus' – not just 'piously', but in a deep theological and doctrinal sense. (Alphonso, 1993)

For the Jesuit, Jesus was the one who went about doing good and telling stories about the Good Samaritan and the Good Shepherd to help people discover for themselves the goodness of God. Now he recognized that Jesus invited him to bring this Christ-meaning to others and that he could do this just by being his true self.

Life and ministry would never be boring again for the Jesuit who found his particular face of Jesus. Our personal identity is the one thing necessary to transform every aspect of our lives, giving it meaning, purpose and direction. It can transform each of us from being a Martha (harassed servant of all) to a Mary (servant of the One in integrated depth). We all need this transformation. Without it the influence of 'who people say we are' can be as powerfully destructive as it was for Jesus, albeit less dramatic. Few of us will hear a crowd baying for our blood, but playing to the crowd can never be what God has in mind for our unique and irreplaceable souls. 'Who do people say that I am?' and 'In what ways am I tempted to play to that opinion?' are good questions for prayerful reflection.

Kathy was a woman of education and a cosmopolitan upbringing. People said that Kathy was a multi-talented and confident woman who could be relied upon for help in every conceivable situation. Moreover, they took full advantage of this; calling on this most neighbourly of neighbours for practical help and moral support morning, noon and night. Kathy, however, found herself feeling somewhat trapped and often exhausted by her many talents and gifts and her earnest desire to serve God and others with them. How, she wondered, could she stop playing 'Jack of all trades' to her family, community and church long enough to discover the one contribution she alone could make to the kingdom?

The answer lay in that second question Jesus asked his companions. She must turn away from what everyone else said about her, to ask Jesus how *he* saw her. That is precisely what she did; 'Who am I, Christ? Who do you say I am?' she prayed. Her mind and heart were drawn instantly to a favourite scripture – the raising of Lazarus and, in her imagination, she pictured the scene at the tomb. However, whereas she usually heard the call to Lazarus to arise, this time what struck her was Jesus saying simply to someone 'move the stone'. Without hesitating, Kathy moved forward. Not, she realized, because here was a task that she could do as well as any other person – and in addition to all the other tasks she carried out – but because *this* was her identity in Christ. She was the stonemover.

It was a sudden revelation, yet as familiar as the palms of her hands. Kathy knew she could not have invented this vocation for herself. For a start, there was nothing particularly attractive about it and it lacked the two things she most often found herself attracted to: a sense of glamour or martyred heroism. Still she could clearly see how it fitted with her experience, her gifts and her understanding of relationships. 'We move obstacles for people in many ways,' she says, 'by loving who they are, by clarifying things they hadn't perceived or understood before.' Suddenly her range of what she thought of as 'non-specific skills' made sense to her. She could look back and see that when God had used her to help another person, effectively all she had been asked to do was use an appropriate skill to move a stone of some sort that obscured Jesus from them.

Alphonso agrees that looking back is one important way of confirming the personal identity:

With a certain thrill of discovery the retreatant 'wakes up' ever more deeply to the fact that the 'Personal vocation' he/she has discerned has been amazingly present in his/her concrete history from the very beginning. It is quite an experience, in fact, to listen to the retreatant as he/she enthusiastically traces the presence of his/her particular 'personal vocation' through the different stages of his/her concrete history. My response to such enthusiastic sharing on the part of the retreatant is always a very quiet comment: 'Are you surprised that your personal vocation has been present all through your life history? If this is truly your personal vocation, then it *should* be present: it was not given to you now in this retreat but, to use the Scriptural phrase, "from your mother's womb" (Cf. Is 49,1: 'The Lord called me from the womb, from the body of my mother he named my name'). You have just "awoken" to it now, you have discovered or "discerned" it now. It was given to you from the beginning.' (Alphonso, 1993)

Having discovered the discoverable, Kathy – like Jesus before her – went off to the desert. Being a mother of two young children, a retreat was out of the question, but Kathy, led by the Holy Spirit, managed to draw apart for an hour each day and used this time to pray about her newly found or remembered identity. As her true trade came into focus so did some important limitations of it.

Her temptation, she quickly realized, was to do more than move stones. The stonemover in the story of Lazarus did not have the power to bring Lazarus to life and out of the tomb. It is Jesus who must raise Lazarus from the dead. However, it was easy for Kathy to confuse the role of moving the stone in someone's life with the task of actually saving that person's soul – or of rescuing them from all trouble and discomfort.

With profound humility (a grace that comes with knowing who we are before God) Kathy recognized that whenever she wants to save people as well as kick their stone away, she invariably ends up moving the stone only to put it (or another like it) back in place! This temptation, along with her natural inclination towards both martyrdom and glamorous feats of acrobatics with her time, talents and energy, needed to be acknowledged – such temptations would come again and again in life, and always attractively dressed like angels of light and messengers of mercy. But there is good news for Kathy and for all of us. We, like Jesus before us, must wrestle with our own temptations, but these can never again be as power-ful as they were before we knew who we are, why we are here, and what paths of virtue God has in mind for us.

So who does Jesus say you are? If your answer is 'a Jack of all trades', then perhaps, like Kathy, your gifts and abilities have taken over and need to be offered in prayer to Jesus so that some focus can be found for them before you collapse with exhaustion! To co-operate with this prayer we need to be honest about our own dreams and desires while at the same time being as available as we can to God's dream for us.

Many people never discover their personal identity (what Alphonso calls the 'personal vocation') because they put no-go areas on their life and availability. If I insist, however unconsciously, that the personal vocation must bring fame, fortune, honour and security – or more modestly, that it pro-vide me with a living, or does/does not necessitate moving from this place, or changing this familiar lifestyle – then I hinder the discovery. Remember that the crowd could not see the identity of Jesus because they wanted him to be Elijah and all that Elijah meant to them. Peter, however, loved Jesus enough to let him be himself.

In addition, if I think I can discover my personal identity without the help of those around whom I live and move and have my being, then I should remember that Jesus needed help from his companions to discover his. Only by living in community with Jesus and others will we discover the aspect of Christ that is our own truest, deepest identity; our way of being Christian. People who say they can be Christian without being part of a Christian community will never discover who they are in Christ. For only in community will we hear the risen Christ ask each of us, 'Who do you say I am?' By answering from our soul we will discover not only who he is for us, but our personal identity in him.

It will fit like a glove, this truth about yourself; it will use your personality, gifts, skills, passions. It will be what you really want, and though it may entail lots of hard work, this will feel like life in all its fullness, at least part of the time. You may make a living by expressing it in some way, as a nurse or doctor might, whose Christ is the One who heals the sick. Or it may bring meaning to employment or unemployment without being so directly connected. For example, 'You are the Christ, the One who calls for true justice' need not be the vocation of a judge or lawyer. It could be the meaning of Christ for a politician or a farmer, or a seller of the *Big Issue*, for a teacher, or industrialist, or a 'home-parent'.

For me, Christ is the One who sets the captives free. This in turn is my identity in him, and regardless of what I do or where I live, this truth of who I am remains. This Christ lives in me. I am called from the deepest, truest, most authentic part of my being to set others free, in casual conversations, in business, in my family, community. Not, I hasten to add, in any heroic or swashbuckling way. While Kathy moves stones for people, I find myself helping good people untie grave-clothes – old images of God, self, and the purpose of life – that

123

cling to them (like the grave-clothes wound tightly round the resurrected Lazarus) and restrict their movement towards Christ.

One thing more is useful to observe. Jesus asks of each of us and of every age: 'Who do you say I am?' The answer we give, both as individuals and as a generation count with him. He will not go beyond our understanding of him. If we say, as previous ages said, that he is Christ the Crusader – or Christ, the one who comes to judge our morals, by his perfect truth – then that is the context in which Christ will operate. Our God is a humble God. If we tell him, as some Christians still do, that he is the one who stands between us and the wrath of God, taking upon himself the punishment we deserve, then from that starting point Christ will work to help us realize the oneness with God that our souls truly enjoy. Christ asks us who we say he is because he is our companion and will walk the road towards wholeness we are already on, starting from the place we are at. At least, this is what belief in the resurrection implies to me. Christ is alive and active in everything, growing with our help in his service to this world. He has always sought, and still seeks, the company of men and women like us and the help we can give with this question of his identity in the here and now of our postmodern age.

References

Alphonso, SJ, Herbert, *The Personal Vocation*. Rome, Centrum Ignatianum Spiritualitatis, 1993.

Peterson, Eugene, *The Message*. Colorado, NavPress Publishing Group, 1993.

11

Anima Christi

> *From that time Jesus began to make it clear to his disciples that he was destined to go to Jerusalem and suffer grievously at the hands of the elders and chief priests and scribes, to be put to death and to be raised up on the third day.*
>
> (Matthew 16.21)

Jesus has a strong hunch that he is the Christ of God, the saviour of this world and every world to come. But discovering his identity was never an end in itself. It was not self-actualization or personal integration that drew him from the carpenter's workshop, but the desire to be of real service to God and to God's world. And not until he puts his life on the line for his hunch will he know for sure. So he prepares to go to Jerusalem for the Passover, knowing that if he is truly himself, the Christ of God, then the things he will say and do there must inevitably bring him into direct conflict with the interests of some very powerful people.

Having discovered who he was and why, Jesus resolves to be faithful to the truth about himself, his relationship to the Father, and the Father's relationship to the world. And for this refusal to be anything other than authentic, he would suffer and die alone and rejected. There the story of Jesus from

Nazareth might have ended, but for the fact that Peter was right when he declared Jesus to be the Son of the Living God. God said so by raising Christ from the dead.

We also must be willing to lose our lives for the sake of the gospel of Jesus Christ. We too are not our own, but souls created by God, for God and for the world. When we know who we are it becomes clear that we are called to lay that person on the line as part of the solution to this world's problems. God is working on wholeness still, and now we are in a position to work with God on the wholeness not of our individual selves, or of a group of individuals like the church, but on the holiness of creation. We are becoming some of those 20 men and women looked for by Thomas Merton; those people who 'see things as they really are . . . who were not dominated or even influenced by any attachment to any created thing or to their own selves or to any gift of God, even to the highest, the most supernaturally pure of His graces' (Merton, 1972). We are the ones 'holding everything together and keeping the universe from falling apart' (Merton, 1972).

Losing our lives in this endeavour is unlikely to mean being killed as Jesus was, but it will certainly mean making the prayer below – a prayer known as 'Anima Christi' (Soul of Christ), and used by Ignatius – our own. It is a prayer of solidarity with the liberating soul of Christ. Take some time to reflect on it, perhaps re-writing it in your own words. Pray it often:

> Jesus, may all that is you flow into me.
> May your body and blood be my food and drink.
> May your passion and death be my strength and life.
> Jesus, with you by my side enough has been given.
> May the shelter I seek be the shadow of your cross.
> Let me not run from the love which you offer,

But hold me safe from the forces of evil.
On each of my dyings shed your light and your love.
Keep calling to me until that day comes,
When, with your saints, I may praise you forever.
Amen.

(Fleming, 1978)

Be warned: this is a dangerous prayer, not one to be mouthed unthinkingly or prayed lightly. For what might happen if the soul of Christ, all that is him, flowed into you? If you did not block this flow or resist its pressure on heart and mind and actions? What would change in life, and what would stay the same if you stopped running away from the love Christ offers in a unique way to you; if what sustained your identity was not anything as transient as health, wealth or reputation, but instead Christ's body (a whole community of people who know their identity in Christ) and the sacraments? This prayer for *kenosis* can transform a follower of Jesus, cell by ambivalent cell, into a disciple of Christ. Though the joys and sorrows of *kenosis* is a lifelong process, here in this prayer is the moment of surrender to it. A moment when we say and really mean, 'Thy kingdom come on earth', beginning with ourselves – me.

If our prayer is answered – if the soul of Christ begins to influence and inform our choices and relationships so that, like Christ, we choose in every situation what is more for the glory of God in us, preferring even to face those many dyings the Anima Christi speaks about than compromise our true selves – then the kingdom might come very soon. What would it look like?

The Old Testament describes the lion lying down with the lamb and swords beaten into pruning hooks, while Jesus told stories of mustard seeds growing into huge trees and of small scraps of yeast transforming a lump of dough into nourishing bread. He spoke quietly of a peaceful revolution where the weak are strong and the strong learn their weakness. Where communion breaks out and community springs up everywhere and in every context as irresistibly individual lives draw together into a perfectly sensible whole; unique and awesome and full of meaning. Jesus called it the kingdom of heaven. Perhaps you find it difficult to imagine the world ever being like this. You wonder how such a thing could ever come about and how God even knows it is in there.

In the early 1950s, on the Japanese island of Koshima, scientists began to provide the *Macaca fuscata* monkey with sweet potatoes dropped in the sand. The monkeys liked this food, but did not like eating the sand that clung to the potatoes. One young monkey solved the difficulty by washing her potato in a stream. She showed her mother how to do this too, then her playmates. The trick was gradually picked up by the others and the scientist observed that in the next six years all the young monkeys learned to wash sandy sweet potatoes before eating them, as did those adults who had children to imitate. Other adults continued to eat their sweet potatoes with sand. By now, however, 99 monkeys from the troop were washing their sweet potatoes. Then one day the hundredth monkey washed a sweet potato, and by evening of the same day all the monkeys were on board, all of them washing the sand away.

Immediately an amazing thing happened. The astounding breakthrough caused by the one-hundredth monkey was not confined to the island of Koshima and the monkeys who had witnessed the spreading practice over the six years. It jumped across the sea to the mainland and a neighbouring island. As the last monkey on Koshima washed a sweet potato, the first monkey on the mainland and on this other island began to wash their sweet potatoes too.

I love this story, and can imagine Jesus using it to teach about the kingdom as he did the parable of the mustard seed. Person by person, soul by soul, the world is being formed into the kingdom. Praying the Anima Christi is dangerous because it is a prayer for this revolution that begins with me. Each of us who prays it earnestly learns to wash away the dust that keeps divinity hidden from our lives. And who knows which one of us, uncovering our truest, deepest identity, our immortal diamond, will trigger a chain reaction resulting in a cosmic breakthrough of the kingdom?

I remember being struck by the global nature of the year 2000 celebrations. Through satellite television the world was able to watch as a new day dawned in every continent, and in many countries on those continents, one after the other. Just as the potato-washing ritual jumped from one island to another, so the 'third millennium' sunrise leapt from nation to nation, courtesy of technology. It began on the island of Samoa. Ironically, this idyllic island is being shrunk because of polluted seas, not something of the Samoans' making. How significant that the world should watch the islanders welcome a new dawn *and* pray for the future of their island. A future that depends on the most developed countries of the world turning away from addictions that cause irreparable harm to our living (and dying) planet. When will we say that enough has been given of economic growth and independence? When will we discover that each of us is immortal diamond – but not alone, not in isolation?

Pierre Teilhard de Chardin describes God's work of wholeness and holiness not as a diamond being uncovered, but of that crystal being formed:

It will not be long before the human mass closes in upon itself and groups all its members in a definitively

129

realised unity. Respect for one and the same law, one and the same orientation, one and the same spirit, are tending to overlay the permanent diversity of individuals and nations. Wait but a little longer, and we shall form but one solid block. The cement is setting.

Already, in the silence of the night, I can hear through this world of tumult a confused rustling as of crystalline needles forming themselves into a pattern or of birds huddling closer together in their nest – a deep murmour of distress, of discomfort, of well-being, of triumph, rising up from the Unity which is reaching its fulfilment. (Lorie and Mascetti, 1997)

I cannot be whole and holy on my own. And there's the rub. The wholeness God has in mind for us is both personal and also universal: a community venture. And while most of us like the idea of a personal identity or vocation in life, we draw back from the real and practical implications of its interconnectivity with all the other unique and irreplaceable beings God has in mind. We in the West cannot be whole and holy while the Samoans watch helplessly as their island home is eroded away. The Christian cannot be whole and holy without the Sikh and the Muslim and the Jew. The rich need the poor even more than the poor need the rich. But, if I am honest, I do not really want to be connected to people I have never met. I balk at the notion that in God's eyes they are connected to me. And I find it frustrating that none of us can live the life God means for us until all of us do.

My reluctance is nothing new. A similar aversion on the part of religious men and women caused tension between them and Jesus of Nazareth. They wanted to believe (and Christians today go on wanting to believe) that holiness could be achieved and maintained by distancing oneself from anything or anyone proscribed by their Law as unholy or impure. But Jesus went to Jerusalem with a quite different message. He prayed for the communion of all people under God: 'Father, may they be one in us, as you are in me and I am in you' (John 17.21). How many of us could say amen to this prayer with sincerity? For us all, God's call to wholeness is as much a stumbling block as a stepping stone.

Consequently, when a person comes for spiritual direction they rarely come with a desire for unity or for *all* that is Christ to start flowing into them. They come instead, like the rich young ruler, to seek personal growth in the Christian life and an integration of their faith with their many activities and roles. It is a good enough starting place, but what is offered to humanity by God is more than this. God is not labouring for my *self*-actualization. When I begin to co-operate with God it very quickly becomes apparent that it is Christ-in-me who is being realized. When I listen to my soul it is Christ's footsteps I hear, his voice inviting me to follow him. The connection God has with me is of cosmic significance, but only because Christ makes it so from the dawn of creation. And listening to my soul is important not only for my life, but for the community of lives touched by my life, because Christ says it is. And one life can transform our world. This is the gospel. It can be our story too. The cement is indeed setting and unity is reaching for fulfilment. Our part in this redemptive crystallization is the discovery of the discoverable: who am I, in Christ? How am I asked to reveal Christ's presence in this world?

Imagine, if you can, what our world would look like if we all discovered the discoverable so that no longer did anyone crave riches, power and honour to make their lives meaningful. What might your family become and what might your community look like? Try to imagine war-torn countries suddenly falling into a peace that lasts because the reasons for conflict don't matter any more. And try to imagine what the super-powers would do with their 'super power' if suddenly they lost interest in the price of oil and winning the next election. How hard is it to imagine a world where we are all free to live a life that in some way expresses who we truly are, and therefore who Christ is for us? How difficult is it to envision a time when our service to the community is valued not because of its glamour or scarcity, but solely on the basis of its authenticity?

My hunch is that you are finding this very hard to imagine. I am too. If we are called to lives of authentic meaning and creativity, will there be road-sweepers in the kingdom I find myself wondering. I can accept (although I cannot imagine it ever happening) the end to despots, but the possible demise of cleansing depots is somehow more difficult. Perhaps because it would impact my life more immediately than world peace ever will. Do I really want what I am praying for when I pray the Anima Christi?

Well, yes and no. I am ambivalent, but then what's new about that? I want to throw my lot in with the soul of Christ. I want to live the life God intends for me while calling others to do the same. But, as usual, I am like the Gerasene demoniac. My name is 'Legion' because when I come to pray for Christ's soul to be the animating principle not only of my life, but of the cosmic life, there are many other voices within me, many other desires holding tenaciously on to me. I want to help others to find their direction in life, but not if it is going to inconvenience me too much. I want world peace but not if it means a lower standard of living, even in the short term. I want everyone to live creative and fulfilling lives, but I hope it doesn't affect the civic amenities I take for granted. There are legions ranged against the soul of Christ.

These legions are hard at work on behalf of the status quo. They resist the flow of Christ, both in me and in the political structures of community life. It is important to open our eyes to the strength of the force opposing Christ; the breadth of its influence and the subtlety of its game plan.

One strategy of this subtle game is to twist the longing we all feel (however ambivalently) for unity into something less revolutionary. When the goal of God's creation is unity, we are in danger of settling for uniformity. God does not understand the concept of uniformity, we only have to look at the diversity of creation to know this. We, however, have difficulty imagining unity and are only too happy to accept any approximation to it that requires less energy to realize. But any movement towards sameness is probably a move away from life in all its fullness for someone. Fascism, religious fundamentalism and racial intolerance are all forms of uniformity – as is the globalization of commerce enslaving the 'Sonias' of our world (see John Pilger's passage in Chapter 8).

We are asked to co-operate with God's work of wholeness by choosing unity over uniformity. In doing so we choose our master, and Jesus himself made it clear that a man or woman can have only one. Prevarication around this matter is itself a choice for the status quo of discrimination. Sitting on the fence is a decision against life in all its fullness.

But the fence looks comfy and compromise appeals to my instinct for survival. What hope is there for my ambivalent self? None whatsoever except through the life, death and resurrection of Jesus Christ. I am called to choose Christ as often as I can, in as many different aspects of my life as I can. I am called and equipped with grace enough to live out of my true and unique self while inviting others, by encouraging word and example, to do the same. I can pray faithfully for the kingdom to come and do my bit towards realizing my

133

petition. I can try to recognize not only my personal Saviour, but also the Saviour of the world, the cosmic Christ, in my own story and in the story of humanity. And I can leave that final miracle of cosmic transformation in the hands of the one whose cosmos it is.

No doubt I will find myself one minute affirmed by God and the next tempted by some resistance in me. Sometimes supported by my companions, and often let down by them. Able to see the bigger picture and to learn from it, then driven into a parochial corner of complacency and ignorance. No doubt I will always need Christ to point to my gifts and identify my compulsions. Again and again I will need to be reminded of my true identity while being forgiven my reluctance to throw caution to the wind in the pursuit of the life in all fullness it promises. But I have no doubt that all of these things will work together for the greater glory of God in whom I live and move and have my unique and irreplaceable being.

And, who knows, I may step off my paths of virtue less often if, like Mary, I have an Elizabeth to accompany me. Someone to give me courage when I am afraid of the demands of Christ's gospel, to point me to my soul and beyond it to the soul of Christ, and to pray for me as Paul did for the church at Ephesus – and as I now do for you:

> Out of his infinite glory, may he give you the power through his Spirit for your hidden self to grow strong, so that Christ may live in your hearts through faith, and then, planted in love and built on love, you will with all the saints have strength to grasp the breadth and the length, the height and the depth; until, knowing the love of Christ, which is beyond all knowledge, you are filled with the utter fullness of God.

Glory be to him whose power, working in us, can do infinitely more than we can ask or imagine; glory be to him from generation to generation in the Church and in Christ Jesus for ever and ever. Amen. (Ephesians 3.16–21)

References

Fleming, SJ, David L., *Draw Me Into Your Friendship: The Spiritual Exercises. A Literal Translation and a Contemporary Reading*. St Louis, Institute of Jesuit Sources, 1996.

Lorie, Peter, and Mascetti, Manuela Dunn (eds), *The Quotable Spirit*. London, Newleaf, 1997.

Merton, Thomas, *Seeds of Contemplation*. Wheathampstead, Anthony Clarke Books, 1972.